The Delaplaine
2022 Long Weekend Guide

Andrew Delaplaine

**NO BUSINESS HAS PAID A SINGLE PENNY OR GIVEN *ANYTHING*
TO BE INCLUDED IN THIS BOOK.**

Senior Writer - **James Cubby**

Copyright © by Gramercy Park Press - All rights reserved.

NEW ORLEANS
The Delaplaine
Long Weekend Guide

TABLE OF CONTENTS

Chapter 1 – WHY NEW ORLEANS? – 5

Chapter 2 – GETTING ABOUT – 11

Chapter 3 – WHERE TO STAY – 13
High on the Hog – Sensible Alternatives – On a Budget

Chapter 4 – WHERE TO EAT – 33
Extravagant – Middle Ground – Budget

Chapter 5 – NIGHTLIFE – 105

Chapter 6 – WHAT TO SEE & DO – 121

Chapter 7 – SHOPPING & SERVICES – 146

INDEX – 150

Chapter 1
WHY NEW ORLEANS?

Only because it's one of the most fascinating cities in America, that's why.

In all my years of travel, I've always maintained that there are only a handful of cities in the U.S. that are thoroughly unique.

Of course, every place is unique *technically,* but what I mean by that is you'd be hard pressed to tell me the difference between Florence, S.C., and Darlington, S.C., if you were to drive through them. Or for that matter Sumter, S.C. Though they're different from each other, they're not *substantially* different. They're Podunk little towns in South Carolina that have nothing to distinguish them except the road that luckily leads you out of them to some more interesting place. (I know. I lived in a town like that when I was a kid. Never again.)

New Orleans is not a town you can say that about.

With its rich cultural diversity (going back to the 1600s) that mixes in the French, the African, the Creole, the Spanish—and a lot of other influences—New Orleans is a fragrant stew of Life.

This is the birthplace of Jazz, which dates back to around 1910. I've always found it puzzling why Jazz is so unknown to younger audiences. It's such an American institution, but it doesn't seem to have found its place among the younger audiences today.

Since Katrina, there have been lots of great new restaurants that have opened, giving the city a food scene that rivals in richness what famous Southern chefs are doing in places like Charleston and Savannah.

And while you're sure to head straight to the French Quarter if this is your first visit, be sure to explore the Garden District if just to see the fabulous houses. You'll wish you lived in one of them.

Next to the French Quarter is the Central Business District (CBD) where the Superdome is located along with lots of museums.

Crime has gone up since Katrina, so you want to beware of certain areas. Ask your hotel or host if you have any questions. Most tourist areas are safe, however. Beware of hustles and pickpockets.

Also, there's a local saying, "Nothing good happens in the Quarter after midnight," and it's true. The bouncers and other security personnel in the clubs can be really nasty when dealing with drunks, and many have been sent to the hospital. Do not argue with them. You will not win.

Even with all my warnings, don't let me give you the impression you should think twice about coming here. You'd be *crazy* not to visit New Orleans if you have the chance. Arriving here always sends your senses into overdrive, into a fever pitch, whether it's your first time here or your tenth or thirtieth.

The uncomfortable muggy summer is the season that for me evokes the true sense of New Orleans. There's something about the town that makes you feel "air conditioning" is wrong. (Although it's a blessed relief to have it—I'm just talking metaphorically.) You wonder how people ever lived in the vortex of sweat and the smell of rotting tropical plants.

Those smells.

The humidity.

The jasmine.

The wrought iron grilles adorning the houses.

The smell of fried seafood.

The different dialects.

The St. Charles Avenue streetcar, still un-air-conditioned after all these years with its open windows and wooden benches.

The cemeteries that are more eerie than any others.

The music, the music, the music.

The rich Uptown lawyers taking their time over 4-hour lunches at Galatoire's while they swill down French burgundy and eat oysters Rockefeller.

The serenity of the Garden District.

The craziness of the Quarter.

It's all just too much. And all too wonderful.

How to say it: Don't use "Nawlins." The best way for an out-of-towner to say it is: *noo-OHR-luhnz*.

Chapter 2
GETTING ABOUT

If you're confining your visit to the French Quarter and the CBD, a car will be more of a hassle than help. You can walk most everywhere, and for slightly longer jaunts, rely on the excellent trolley cars, buses and taxis to get around.

Tourist Information: www.neworleansonline.com

Chapter 3
WHERE TO STAY

ACE HOTEL
600 Carondelet St, 504-900-1180
https://www.acehotel.com/neworleans/
NEIGHBORHOOD: Warehouse District
Everything about this fashionable 234 room hotel and slick and smart, from the gorgeous rooftop pool, with lots of greenery softening the lounging area, to the creatively designed lobby. The bars & restaurants here attract not just tourists, but a lot of locals, because the place is so hot & trendy (like all Ace Hotels). The rooms, I'll have to warn you, are somewhat Spartan for my tastes. Not quaint. Not Southern, Not charming. Which is fine if you don't plan on spending any time in them. The public rooms are the most fun. Amenities: complimentary Wi-Fi and flat-screen TVs. On site features: 3 restaurants, bar/lounge, poolside bar, outdoor pool, rooftop bar, and 24-hour fitness center. Smoke-free hotel. Upscale suites have living rooms with turntables and acoustic guitars. Located in the Warehouse District just a short walk from Bourbon Street. Pet-friendly.

AUDUBON COTTAGES
509 Dauphine St, New Orleans, 800-935-8740
www.auduboncottages.com
NEIGHBORHOOD: French Quarter

This collection of 7 antique-filled romantic cottages dating back to the early 1800s you'll find sequestered behind an unobtrusive gate. Lush landscaping is one of the nice things about this place. The exposed brick walls remind you that some of these cottages were formerly slave quarters. Each lodging has its own full wet bar, fridge, coffee maker and ice maker and private patios. John James Audubon completed his masterwork, "Audubon's Birds of America," while staying here in 1821. (There's a handsome copy in each cottage.) Butler / concierge service on site to handle any special needs you might have. Amenities include: flat-screen TVs, Wi-Fi access, free coffee, tea & soft drinks, and free continental breakfast. Shared salt-water pool – said to be the oldest pool in New Orleans.

THE COLUMNS
3811 St Charles Ave, New Orleans, 504-899-9308
www.thecolumns.com
NEIGHBORHOOD: Milan
Built in 1883, this grand hotel is both elegant and modern mixing old world décor with modern amenities and is considered one of the grandest interiors in the city. The Columns offers 20 beautifully furnished guestrooms on two levels. Amenities include: full Southern breakfast, free daily newspaper and live jazz in the Ballroom. you enter the **Victorian Lounge** through 12-foot-high solid mahogany doors that take you into the bar with 15-foot-high ceilings. You can sit on rocking chairs on the porch that overlook the St. Charles, which makes this excellent for people-watching. Conveniently

located near the St Charles streetcar line and near shopping, restaurants, galleries, and nightlife.

GREEN HOUSE INN
1212 Magazine St, New Orleans, 504-525-1333
www.thegreenhouseinn.com
NEIGHBORHOOD: Lower Garden District; Warehouse District
This small historic inn offers a beautiful Lower Garden District setting. Built in 1840 as a Greek Revival side-hall townhouse, the Inn has 9 intimate guestrooms. Amenities include the clothing optional tree-shaped therapeutic salt-water swimming pool, an oversized Jacuzzi-style Hot tub, free Wi-Fi, reading library, free Continental breakfast, and flat screen TVs. Free off-street parking. Conveniently located to the French Quarter, the Garden District, the Warehouse/Arts District and local attractions.

HARRAH'S NEW ORLEANS
228 Poydras St, New Orleans, 800-427-7247
www.caesars.com/harrahs-new-orleans
NEIGHBORHOOD: Warehouse District
Just outside the French Quarter you'll find this upscale casino 450-room hotel in a 26-story building with a 24/7 casino. The hotel offers plush modern rooms. There's nothing "charming" about it. You'd stay here because you want to spend time in the casino and because it's easy. Amenities include: free Wi-Fi, flat-screen TVs, and mini-fridges. Hotel features include: Fitness Center with gym, 2 casual seafood restaurants, a Creole spot, a pub, a coffee

shop, a 12-lane bowling alley, a lounge with live music and a bar. Non-smoking hotel.

HENRY HOWARD HOTEL
2041 Prytania St, New Orleans, 504-313-1577
www.henryhowardhotel.com
NEIGHBORHOOD: Lower Garden District
Housed in a majestic "double-gallery" 1867 mansion built for a steamship owner, this chic hotel in the wonderfully quiet of the Lower Garden District a short ride from the noisy French Quarter offers a variety of 18 comfortably (and creatively) furnished rooms from singles to an airy 3-bedroom suite. Magazine Street's collection of restaurants, antique shops and bars is just a short walk away. The Queen Superior rooms are not very big, so book a Royal Queen room. Amenities: Complimentary Wi-Fi and flat-screen TVs. Some rooms have sitting areas and balconies. Lobby bar but no on site restaurant. (There are plenty on Magazine Street nearby.) Smoke-free hotel.

HOTEL JUNG
1500 Canal St, New Orleans, 504-226-5864
www.junghotel.com
NEIGHBORHOOD: Central Business District
Upmarket hotel in a remodeled 1920s building. The color scheme here is gray and sand. So it's very soothing. Rooms and suites are unusually large, with marble floors. Rooms include kitchenettes, washer/dryers, complimentary Wi-Fi and flat-screen TVs. On-site Art Deco restaurant serving Creole fare.

Complimentary breakfast. Outdoor pool and fitness center. Pet-friendly. Smoke-free hotel.

HOTEL LE MARAIS
717 Conti St, New Orleans, 504-525-2300
www.hotellemarais.com
NEIGHBORHOOD: French Quarter
This upscale boutique hotel offers a mixture of classic and modern charm with 66 plush guestrooms. Amenities include: 42-inch flat screen TV, free high-speed Internet access, two free bottles of water, free daily newspaper, walk-in showers, wake-up service, free Continental breakfast, valet parking, and state-of-the-art fitness center. Conveniently located near the city's best restaurants, art galleries and shopping.

HOTEL MAZARIN
730 Bienville St, New Orleans, 504-581-7300
www.hotelmazarin.com
NEIGHBORHOOD: French Quarter
This new luxury boutique hotel offers 102 spacious rooms perfectly suited for the modern traveler. Amenities include: free breakfast, 100% smoke-free environment, 42" flat screen TVs, wake-up service, free high-speed Internet access, free bottled water, and MP3 Docking Station. Conveniently located in the popular French Quarter near local attractions, restaurants, shopping, and nightlife.

HOTEL MONTELEONE
214 Royal St, New Orleans, 504-523-3341,
www.hotelmonteleone.com
NEIGHBORHOOD: French Quarter
This luxury hotel, one of New Orleans landmarks since 1886, offers 600 guest rooms with 55 luxury

suites and literary author suites. Many of the beautiful rooms feature high ceilings, crown molding and traditional décor. **The Carousel Bar** here was a legendary hangout for celebrities like Truman Capote, Tennessee Williams, William Faulkner and Eudora Welty. Its circus theme and hand-painted wooden chairs evoke another era, but only when it's not filled with tourists who flock here so early they're waiting in line an hour before the place opens. The best time here is late in the evenings on week nights, not weekends, when it's loud & raucous. Amenities include: heated rooftop pool, 24-hour fitness center, full-service spa, valet parking, and LCD TVs. Conveniently located near local attractions, restaurants, shopping and nightlife. This is a non-smoking and pet friendly hotel.

HOTEL PETER & PAUL
2317 Burgundy St, 504-356-5200
www.hotelpeterandpaul.com
NEIGHBORHOOD: Faubourg Marigny District
Set in a former church and school, this upscale hotel features elegant rooms furnished in antiques. There's something about the drapes they use that puts me back in the 19th Century every time I walk into this place. The "church" atmosphere might have something to do with that as well. Loaded down with charm and history. Amenities: complimentary Wi-Fi, flat-screen TVs, complimentary newspapers. On-site features: restaurant, bar/lounge, coffee shop/café and fitness center with gym. Smoke-free hotel. Six-minute walk from tram stop.

HOUMAS HOUSE PLANTATION & GARDENS
40136 Hwy 942, Darrow, 225-473-9380
www.houmashouse.com
Located on a lush 38-acre plantation, the Gardens of Houmas House offers a luxurious and romantic getaway. The cottages are decorated with old world furnishings similar to the lavish lifestyle of the wealthy barons of the early 1800s. Amenities include: free breakfast and tour of the mansion. Two onsite restaurants. Enjoy beautiful gardens, the Neptune Pavilion Fountain, and Fountain Courtyard.

INTERNATIONAL HOUSE
221 Camp St, New Orleans, 504-553-9550
www.ihhotel.com
NEIGHBORHOOD: Central Business District
This chic 117-room hotel is located in a restored Beaux-Arts bank building. There's a nice lounge called **LOA**, which takes its name from the kindlier spirits in voodoo. Lots of candles give the place a

pleasant laid-back mood. It's about a 10-minute walk to the middle of the French Quarter, so you're far enough away from the beer-swilling faux-hippies that you see so many of in the Quarter. Amenities include: flat screen TVs, stereos, free Wi-Fi, and Aveda bath amenities. Penthouses and rooms with terraces are available. Smoke-free hotel. Conveniently located near the St Charles Avenue Streetcar line and French Quarter.

MAISON DE LA LUZ
546 Carondelet St, 504-814-7720
https://maisondelaluz.com/
NEIGHBORHOOD: Business and arts district
Upscale guest house/hotel, from the people who own the Ace Hotels, featuring 67 luxury suites. While the Ace hotels always throw off an intentional hip modern vibe, here you'll get gussied up reimagined Southern charm with a lot of modern twists. You enter through stately white columns out front and pass into a lobby unlike any you've seen before. You'll love the extra high ceilings in the rooms, the little touches they've made to the décor that highlight certain architectural details, the trompe l'oeil wallpaper & the charming décor in the Breakfast Room, the intricate design in the rugs of the Living Room in the lobby, the daily tea & coffee service, the hand-crafted furniture that makes each room quite a bit different from the others, and a lot more. It's one of the most originally conceived designs I've seen in a while, from the black-and-white checkered floors to the fringe on the chairs in the lobby. It's a bit away from all those trashy people flocking to the French

Quarter (which later in the evening might even include you, LOL). Amenities: complimentary Wi-Fi and Continental breakfast. On-site features: restaurant, bar, and fitness center. Smoke-free hotel. Pet-friendly. Conveniently located near Lafayette Square.

THE OLD NO. 77
535 Tchoupitoulas St, New Orleans, 504-527-5271
www.old77hotel.com
NEIGHBORHOOD: Warehouse Arts District
Located just three blocks from the French Quarter, this boutique hotel is a favorite of art lovers and cultural adventurers. You'll love the hardwood floors and old brick walls (the building dates back to 1854). Rooms decorated with a mix of rustic and modern flair. They not only have an art gallery that puts the spotlight on local artists, but a restaurant from Top Chef contestant Nina Compton. Amenities include: flat-screen TVs and coffeemakers. The resort fee includes high-speed Wi-Fi, continental breakfast and access to the fitness center.

THE ROOSEVELT
130 Roosevelt Way, New Orleans, 504-648-1200
www.rooseveltneworleans.com
NEIGHBORHOOD: Central Business District
A luxury Waldorf Astoria property located in a beautiful 1863 building, the Roosevelt offers 504 plush guestrooms in one of the most historic landmarks in the city. (It's come off a major renovation, so everything here is shipshape.) Amenities include: 42-inch flat-screen TVs, Wi-Fi access, and iPod docks. Located just one block from Bourbon Street. Hotel features include: an upscale Italian restaurant, a lounge with a raw bar, a coffee shop, full-service spa, fitness center and the historic

Sazerac Bar, which still has its original Art Deco glass and Paul Ninas murals on display, alone with the stop-over. Of course, while visiting, you'll have to sample the signature cocktail the bar takes its name from.

ROYAL SONESTA HOTEL
300 Bourbon St, New Orleans, 504-586-0300
www.sonesta.com
NEIGHBORHOOD: French Quarter
This 4 Diamond approved hotel offers 483 guest rooms and 35 luxurious suites with beautiful views of the French Quarter, the pool and patio terrace or the lush tropical courtyard. Amenities include: flat screen TVs, high-speed Internet access, and a smoke-free environment. The hotel includes the R Club, the private hotel within a hotel on the 7th floor with private key access. Onsite venues include: Desire Bistro & Oyster Bar, PJ's Coffee Café, Irvin

Mayfield's Jazz Playhouse, Restaurant R'evolution, and Le Booze on Bourbon. Conveniently located within walking distance to the Mississippi Riverfront, the Central Business District ant world famous attractions.

ROYAL STREET INN AND R BAR
1431 Rue Royal, New Orleans, 504-948-7499
www.royalstreetinn.com
NEIGHBORHOOD: Marigny
This Inn offers what they like to call "sleazy luxury." A stay at this Inn is more an experience than just a night at the Inn. The onsite **R Bar** is usually packed with colorful locals and since in this case B&B stands for bed and beverage, guests are entitled to two free cocktails. Amenities include: TV/DVDs, MP3 docking station, and free Wi-Fi. Just a few blocks from the French Quarter.

THE SAINT
931 Canal St, New Orleans, 504-522-5400
https://www.marriott.com/hotels
NEIGHBORHOOD: Central Business District
This French Quarter gem located in a century-old building offers comfortable accommodations for the experienced traveler. The **Burgundy Bar** usually offers live music 7 singers. The on-site eatery, **Tempt**, is very good, and features rotating artworks by local artists. Amenities include: 46" flat screen HDTV, free Wi-Fi high speed Internet Access, valet parking (additional fee), lobby pool table and Burgundy bar. Conveniently located for local

attractions, shopping, restaurants, festivals, and nightlife.

ST. PHILIP RESIDENCE
612 St. Philip St., New Orleans, 504-523-2197
https://saintphilipresidence.com/#info
NEIGHBORHOOD: French Quarter
When you want the experience staying in true old New Orleans, the St. Philip is the place! Nothing like a traditional hotel, the St. Philip is a small, private retreat located right in the heart of the French Quarter. You'll be in very good company as their list of former guests reads like a who's who, "Residental quality

apartments and a management staff that's just as colorful as the building itself."

SHERATON NEW ORLEANS
500 Canal St, New Orleans, 504-525-2500
www.sheratonneworleans.com/
NEIGHBORHOOD: Central Business District
After a $50 million revitalization, this Sheraton offers 1,110 non-smoking guestrooms including 53 suites. Pretty much anywhere you go you'll be able to see their towering building, so you'll never get lost. Amenities include: in-room movies and video games, cable TV, wake-up service, wired & wireless high speed Internet access (available for a fee), fitness center, club lounge, and valet parking. Conveniently located near local restaurants, nightlife, and attractions.

SONIET HOUSE
1133 Chartres St, New Orleans, 504-522-0570
www.soniathouse.com
NEIGHBORHOOD: French Quarter
Set in 3 French Colonial cottages from the 1830s, this elegant hotel offers traditionally decorated rooms and suites. Amenities include: free Wi-Fi, flat-screen TVs with cable, mini-fridges, and free continental breakfast. Hotel features include: lush courtyards, fountains, and 2 outdoor pools. Located minutes from Bourbon Street and the French Market.

TERRELL HOUSE
1441 Magazine St, New Orleans, 504-237-2076
www.terrellhouse.com
NEIGHBORHOOD: Lower Garden District
Built in 1857, this charming bed and breakfast offers 12 beautifully appointed gust rooms and suites. Amenities include: cable TV, wireless Internet, and most have views of the lush courtyard. All rooms have private baths. Conveniently located near local attractions, restaurants, shopping, and nightlife.

W NEW ORLEANS
316 Chartres St, New Orleans, 504-581-1200
www.wfrenchquarter.com
NEIGHBORHOOD: French Quarter
This beautifully decorated hotel offers 97 guest rooms including 4 studio suites and 1 deluxe suite. The design of the hotel celebrates the jazz age and the rooms are welcoming with the W signature beds and W exclusive Bliss Bath amenities. Other amenities include: courtyard pool, on-site restaurant (from the same company that owns the **Commander's Palace**) and bar, fitness center, whatever/whenever service, doorman, dry cleaning service, outdoor pool, and daily weekday newspaper. Within walking distance to live jazz, bistros, boutiques and the iconic Jackson Square. Pet-friendly hotel.

WINDSOR COURT
300 Gravier St, New Orleans, 800-262-2662
www.windsorcourthotel.com
NEIGHBORHOOD: Central Business District
This luxury hotel offers the best in accommodations and Southern hospitality. The Windsor Court features 316 non-smoking guest rooms and suites, each with its own character and charm. Amenities include: rooftop pool and deck, fitness center, 24-hour suite service, free wireless and wired high-speed Internet, full-service spa, and valet laundry service. The hotel offers a variety of in-house restaurants and lounges including: the **Grill Room**, **Polo Club Lounge**, and the **Cocktail Bar at the Windsor Court**, all featuring live music. Traditional afternoon tea is served in **Le Salon**. (In the Grill Room, get the Andouille-and-crayfish omelette and the excellent beignets.) You'll find a lot of local hanging out at the lobby bar, whether it's the cocktail craft crowd or the businessman dropping in for a drink after work.

Conveniently located near local shopping, restaurants, museums, and nightlife.

WYNDHAM LA BELLE MAISON
209 Magazine St, New Orleans, 504-558-5900
www.wyndham-vr-la-belle-maison.hotelsofneworleans.net/en
NEIGHBORHOOD: Central Business District. This resort offers the ultimate vacation destination. Here you'll find a mixture of relaxed elegance and modern charm. This time-share brings together 3 separate buildings to make up 130 rooms, ranging from small studios to expansive 2-bedroom suites. All have little kitchens. Amenities include: outdoor saltwater spa, indoor hot tub and sauna, exercise room, and massage services (available upon request). This is a non-smoking resort. Conveniently located to local attractions, restaurants, theaters, galleries, shopping and nightlife.

Chapter 4
WHERE TO EAT

1000 FIGS
3141 Ponce de Leon St., 504-301-0848
https://www.1000figs.com/
CUISINE: Falafel / Middle Eastern
DRINKS: No Booze
SERVING: Lunch & Dinner; Closed Sundays
PRICE RANGE: $$
NEIGHBORHOOD: Mid-City

Small eatery with bleached wooden floors, spare wooden tables and mismatching wooden chairs make you think WOOD. The place is softened by some strategically placed plants perched on some shelves and these little plant-like tendrils hanging from the light fixtures. None of this matters, however, because the place is very popular, so be prepared to wait at peak times. Order from the counter and take a number so the server can find you. Sit at one of the few tables out front if you can snag one. Favorites: Lamb & Pork Kofta Kebab; Mint Adjika Braised Lamb Platter; Falafel Platter. Great for sharing.

ACME OYSTER HOUSE
724 Iberville St, New Orleans, 504-522-5973
www.acmeoyster.com
CUISINE: Seafood
DRINKS: Full Bar
SERVING: Lunch, Dinner
PRICE RANGE: $$

NEIGHBORHOOD: French Quarter
For more than 100 years this New Orleans eatery has been offering up delicious seafood dishes. Menu favorites include the fresh, hand-shucked oysters and Seafood Gumbo. There's often a wait for tables but it's worth it just to see the shuckers do their thing. On a stage this would be called performance art.

Veggie sampler at Addis Nola

ADDIS NOLA
422 S Broad St, New Orleans, 504-218-5321
https://www.addisnola.com/
CUISINE: Ethiopian / Comfort Food
DRINKS: Beer & Wine
SERVING: Lunch & Dinner
PRICE RANGE: $$
NEIGHBORHOOD: Tulane / Gravier
Not just new, but one of only two Ethiopian restaurants in Louisiana. Offering a menu of authentic Ethiopian cuisine, like Inerja, a popular flatbread. The sides are excellent and flavorful—cabbage with carrots, yellow split peas, red lentils. My Favorites:

Spicy Beef Ribs and Veggie Combo. Vegetarian offerings.

ANCORA PIZZERIA
4508 Freret St, New Orleans, 504-324-1636
www.ancorapizza.com
CUISINE: Pizza
DRINKS: Full Bar
SERVING: Dinner
PRICE RANGE: $$
NEIGHBORHOOD: Uptown/Freret
This pizzeria serves authentic Neapolitan pizzas and house-made salumi. The *arancini* (Sicilian fried rice balls coated with breadcrumbs) is wildly good. They also offer a great selection of Italian wines and hand-crafted cocktails. Closed Sundays.

ARNAUD'S
813 Bienville Ave, New Orleans, 504-523-5433
www.arnaudsrestaurant.com
CUISINE: Cajun/Creole
DRINKS: Full Bar

SERVING: Dinner
PRICE RANGE: $$$
NEIGHBORHOOD: French Quarter
Located just off Bourbon Street, this legendary eatery is the picture image of what you think of when you think of New Orleans, with its tile floor and the wrought iron porches. They serve classic Creole cuisine in an elegant atmosphere. The main dining room offers the perfect setting for romantic dinner and guests can enjoy live Dixieland Jazz in the **Jazz Bistro**. Menu favorites include: Rainbow Trout with Creole Sauce and Arnaud's Crab Cakes.

ATCHAFALAYA
901 Louisiana Ave, New Orleans, 504-891-9626
www.atchafalayarestaurant.com
CUISINE: Cajun/Creole
DRINKS: Full Bar
SERVING: Dinner nightly, Lunch daily except Tues & Wed
PRICE RANGE: $$
NEIGHBORHOOD: East Riverside
Some come for the build your own Bloody Mary bar. However, it's the food that keeps them coming back. Menu favorites include: Fried Chicken N Biscuits, eggs "treme" (they use crawfish in this dish) and Shrimp & Grits. Save room for the Blue Cheese Flan made with reduced balsamic and pumpkin seed brittle.

AUGUST
301 Tchoupitoulas St, New Orleans, 504-299-9777
www.restaurantaugust.com

CUISINE: French / Creole
DRINKS: Full Bar
SERVING: Dinner nightly; Lunch on Friday
PRICE RANGE: $$$$
NEIGHBORHOOD: Central Business District
Chef John Besh offers a creative menu of French cuisine in a beautifully decorated 19th century space. Striking chandeliers hang from high ceilings in this charming eatery. Brick walls are buttressed by ornate columns, giving the place an air of authority. Menu favorites include: Smoke swordfish cru and Crispy branzino with royal red shrimp. Or one of my favorites, the chili-enhanced soft shell crab. Reservations recommended.

BAKERY BAR
1179 Annunciation St, New Orleans, 504-210-8519
www.bakery.bar
CUISINE: Desserts
DRINKS: Full Bar
SERVING: Lunch, Dinner
PRICE RANGE: $$
NEIGHBORHOOD: Lower Garden District
Unique neighborhood spot with a bakery inspired menu and craft cocktails. Everything from cookies to cakes and cheese and charcuterie boards. There's a local favorite—the 7-layer "doberge" cake, with multiple flavors like cinnamon and chocolate. Board gamers paradise.

BARROW'S CATFISH
8300 Earhart Blvd #103, New Orleans, 504-265-8995
https://www.barrowscatfish.com/
CUISINE: Seafood
DRINKS: No Booze
SERVING: Lunch & Dinner, Closed Sun
PRICE RANGE: $$$
NEIGHBORHOOD: Gert Town
Serving excellent seafood cuisine since 1943, their menu has a definite Creole twist. Rough brick walls give the place a rustic feel. The biggest seller is their catfish, for which they are rightly famous worldwide. It's just lighted covered with cornmeal before it's flash fried and served hot. Melts in your mouth. My Other Favorites: Chargrilled Oysters (so tasty); Fried

shrimp that is so light and tender; an excellent Gumbo. Try the Bananas Foster Cake for dessert.

BEVI SEAFOOD CO
236 Carrollton Ave, New Orleans, 504-488-7503
www.beviseafoodco.com
CUISINE: Seafood/Sandwiches
DRINKS: Full bar
SERVING: Lunch & Dinner – Tues – Sat; Lunch only Sun & Mon
PRICE RANGE: $$
NEIGHBORHOOD: Mid-City
Market and restaurant in simple surroundings. Menu offers fresh fish, oysters and excellent po'boys. Try their combo – high po-boy and cup of soup. Or go for the Peacemaker, a big po'boy that includes Louisiana fried shrimp, roast beef & Swiss cheese.

THE BON TON CAFÉ
401 Magazine St, New Orleans, 504-524-3386
WEBSITE DOWN AT PRESSTIME
CUISINE: Cajun / Creole
DRINKS: Full Bar
SERVING: Lunch & Dinner; closed Sat & Sun
PRICE RANGE: $$$
NEIGHBORHOOD: Central Business District
Open since 1953, this quaint eatery offers a menu of classic Cajun dishes. Favorites include the Turtle soup, the shrimp and crab okra gumbo and the Crawfish Jambalaya. Get out your Crystal hot sauce. Save room for their delicious Bread pudding.

BRIGTSEN'S
723 Dante St, New Orleans, 504-861-7610
brigtsens.com
CUISINE: Cajun / Creole / Southern
DRINKS: Full Bar
SERVING: Dinner, Closed Sun & Mon
PRICE RANGE: $$$
NEIGHBORHOOD: Leonidas
Modern Creole eatery located in a quaint Victorian cottage. What the chef and his wife do here is quite remarkable: they merged (it's called "fusion" these days) Cajun cuisine from the countryside and bayou

wetlands with elements of Creole cuisine more commonly found in the city. From this unique perspective, they created such dishes as Rabbit Andouille Gumbo; the breaded and quickly fried rabbit is my absolute favorite; Pork Chops served with potato hash sweetened with tasso; Parmesan-crusted Gulf fish with a dollop of crab meat on top of it; Roasted Tripletail Amandine; BBQ Seasoned Redfish with Chipotle Grits Cake. The Southern-inspired desserts are just as novel as their main plates, so save some room for them. Reservations recommended.

BORGNE
601 Loyola Ave, New Orleans, 504-613-3860
www.borgnerestaurant.com
CUISINE: Seafood/American/Southern
DRINKS: Full Bar
SERVING: Lunch, Dinner
PRICE RANGE: $$$
NEIGHBORHOOD: Central Business District
This is a favorite destination for local seafood and Southern dishes. It's a very simple room, big and open and airy, and sends off the same vibe you get at the fish camps that you run across when traveling along the waterways. Menu favorites include: Louisiana White Shrimp Risotto, a spicy shrimp rémoulade, Stuffed Flounder and Sheepshead Fish in a Bag. The desserts are also worth trying like the Lime Ice Box Parfait and the Chocolate Hazelnut Puddin.

BOUCHERIE
8115 Jeannette St, New Orleans, 504-862-5514
www.boucherie-nola.com
CUISINE: Barbeque/Southern
DRINKS: Full Bar
SERVING: Lunch, Dinner
PRICE RANGE: $$
NEIGHBORHOOD: Uptown
One would never think that this Southern-flavored bistro began its life as a food truck. The menu is quite inventive with dishes like Boudin balls and Krispy Kreme bread pudding. Menu favorites include: Blackened shrimp with grit toast and Wagyu Beef Brisket.

BOULIGNY TAVERN
3641 Magazine St, New Orleans, 504-891-1810
www.boulignytavern.com

CUISINE: Tapas/Small Plates
DRINKS: Full Bar
SERVING: Dinner, Late night
PRICE RANGE: $$
NEIGHBORHOOD: East Riverside
This relaxed eatery is basically a gastropub that offers small-plate dining. Menu favorites include croquettes with chorizo and comte, gouda beignets and meatball flatbread. They also offer an impressive list of selected wines and a well-crafted cocktail menu with exotic drink specialties like the Sage Julep. Closed Sundays.

BOURBON HOUSE
144 Bourbon St, New Orleans, 504-522-0111
www.bourbonhouse.com
CUISINE: Cajun/Creole
DRINKS: Full Bar
SERVING: Lunch, Dinner
PRICE RANGE: $$$
NEIGHBORHOOD: French Quarter
Chef Dickie Brennan is well known in New Orleans and offers a menu of great Cajun/Creole cuisine. Menu favorites include: New Orleans Style BBQ Shrimp and Redfish on the Half Shell, though I'm especially fond of the oysters with caviar and Parmesan. This is truly a fine dining experience. And for the bourbon, this place offers an impressive selection of small batch and single barrel bourbons. If you're a bourbon fan, you must try the Frozen Bourbon Milk Punch—it's basically a milkshake, but one you won't soon forget.

BRENNAN'S
417 Royal St, 504-525-9711
https://www.brennansneworleans.com/
CUISINE: Cajun/Creole
DRINKS: Full Bar
SERVING: Breakfast, Lunch, & Dinner
PRICE RANGE: $$$
NEIGHBORHOOD: French Quarter

Most fine dining places aren't open for breakfast, but this one is. This upscale establishment located in a distinctive pinkish 2-level building has been known (since they opened in 1946) for its hearty Creole cuisine. Everybody remembers the lively murals in its main dining room. In good weather, there's a nice courtyard where you can lunch or dine. (Really pretty at night, magical.) Observe the turtles sunbathing on rocks in the little pool. (They don't use those turtles for the Turtle Soup they serve inside, or I hope they don't.) Great spot for breakfast (get the eggs Sardou, with artichokes & poached eggs smothered in Hollandaise). Favorites: BBQ Shrimp Quenelles; Blackened Redfish; Rabbit (crispy skin); Garlic Prawns. Bananas Foster dessert (which was invented here) is a must, and it's prepared tableside, the way it's supposed to be. Reservations recommended. Delicious fresh juices.

BROUSSARD'S
819 Conti St, New Orleans, 504-581-3866
www.broussards.com
CUISINE: Seafood, French, and Cajun/Creole
DRINKS: Full Bar
SERVING: Lunch, Dinner
PRICE RANGE: $$$
NEIGHBORHOOD: French Quarter
A New Orleans fixture for nearly a century, Broussard's offers a menu that mixes French and Creole influences. Here you'll get a dining experience that you won't forget. Menu favorites include: Oven Baked Dover Sole and Gulf Shrimp Lean Lafitte. Desserts are tasty too with selections like Crepes Broussard and the Bananas Foster.

BYWATER AMERICAN BISTRO
2900 Chartres St, 504-605-3827
http://bywateramericanbistro.com/

CUISINE: American (New)
DRINKS: Full Bar
SERVING: Dinner, Brunch on Sat & Sun, Closed on Mon & Tues.
PRICE RANGE: $$
NEIGHBORHOOD: Bywater
Busy eatery where you can see into the open kitchen from your seat at the bar to watch the cooks toiling away under a row of big gleaming copper pots dangling from the ceiling. Old brick walls with wood accents. A chest-high divider separates the bar from the dining room. This is a popular Brunch destination. Favorites: Jerk Chicken Rice; Crispy Hogs Head Boudin; Chicken liver parfait; Rabbit Curry; Kimchi fried rice; Hot Sausage, Egg & Cheese Sandwich (brunch only). Reservations recommended. Small cocktail menu is worthy a second look.

CAFÉ SBISA
1011 Decatur St, New Orleans, 504-522-5565
www.cafesbisanola.com
CUISINE: Southern/Seafood
DRINKS: Full Bar
SERVING: Dinner, Lunch on Sun; Closed Mon & Tues
PRICE RANGE: $$
NEIGHBORHOOD: French Quarter
Ornately decorated venue offering classic (and expertly prepared) French-Creole cuisine since 1899. They had lots of damage during Hurricane Katrina, but recovered eventually. Check out the daily gumbos—they're great whatever the day happens to

be. Favorites: Turtle soup and Louisiana Blue Crab Cakes. Nice wine selection.

CANE & TABLE
1113 Decatur St, New Orleans, 504-581-1112
www.caneandtablenola.com
CUISINE: Caribbean
DRINKS: Full Bar
SERVING: Dinner
PRICE RANGE: $$
NEIGHBORHOOD: French Quarter
This eatery has an old-world ambience (what you might imagine a Colonial-era pub or inn might feel like) with a menu of primarily small plates. Favorites include their delicious ribs soaked in El Dorado rum, braised in ginger, garlic, peppers. The ribs are then battered and deep-fried, which gives you a crispy shell surrounding the succulent meat. The craft cocktails emphasize good aged rums and employ house-made syrups to finish them off perfectly.

CASAMENTO'S
4330 Magazine St, New Orleans, 504-895-9761
www.casamentosrestaurant.com
CUISINE: Seafood
DRINKS: Full Bar
SERVING: Lunch daily, Dinner Thurs. – Sat; closed Sun
PRICE RANGE: $$
NEIGHBORHOOD: East Riverside
Cut little seafood eatery, open since 1919, that's a little off the beaten path but worth the search. Cash-

only spot serves fresh oysters & other seafood in a compact, mosaic-tiled space.

CHARLIE'S STEAK HOUSE
4510 Dryades St, New Orleans, 504-895-9323
https://charliessteakhousenola.com/
CUISINE: Steakhouse
DRINKS: Full Bar
SERVING: Dinner, Closed Sun & Mon
PRICE RANGE: $$$
NEIGHBORHOOD: Uptown
Since 1932, this old-fashioned steakhouse has been serving thick-cut steaks and classic sides. Popular with locals. Forget all about Smith & Wollensky, Del Frisco's, Peter Lugar, the Palm or Ruth's Chris—those famous steakhouses with the tufted leather booths, the dark paneling, the air of mega-deals being made in hushed whispers. No, this is strictly a working class steakhouse. From the outside it looks like a beat-up old pool hall. Inside, it doesn't look much different. But no pool hall ever had food like

this. My Favorites: NY Strip and a Large T-Bone that weighs in at 32 oz. I always get the Crabmeat au Gratin to share with someone. So yummy. Impressive wine list. Reservations recommended.

COCHON BUTCHER
930 Tchoupitoulas St, New Orleans, 504-588-7675
www.cochonbutcher.com
CUISINE: Sandwiches
DRINKS: Full Bar
SERVING: Lunch, Dinner
PRICE RANGE: $$
NEIGHBORHOOD: Central Business District
No-frills butcher shop offering a great selection of sandwiches, with an emphasis on the muffuletta, which they serve hot unless you order it cold. The chef has a special oven to heat them, using a combination of steam and heat that melts the cheese to highlight the flavors of the meat. Try the Le Pig Mac – their version of the Big Mac and the Duck Pastrami Slider. Butcher counter with selection of meats. Le Pig Mac, the mac and cheese and blueberry cheesecake. Menu favorites include: Buckboard Bacon Melt and Roasted Turkey with Arugula, Tomato and Fontina. The butcher shop offers in-house made meats, terrines, sausages, and fresh cut meats. Great place for catering needs. No reservations.

COMMANDER'S PALACE
1403 Washington Ave, New Orleans, 504-899-8221
www.commanderspalace.com
CUISINE: Cajun/Creole
DRINKS: Full Bar
SERVING: Lunch, Dinner
PRICE RANGE: $$$$
NEIGHBORHOOD: Garden District

This place gets as much hype as a tourist trap but there's a difference: this is the "Real Thing." In a classic Victorian setting, this eatery offers a menu that combines modern New Orleans cooking with Haute Creole. This is the place decades ago where French Creole and Cajun were first blended with nouvelle cuisine. There have been many copycats, and many of them are very good, but this place still sets a very high bar. Though the place can be quite expensive, one tip followed frequently by locals is to head here for lunch on weekdays when it's always very cheap. Menu favorites include: Pecan Crusted Gulf Fish, Absinthe Poached Oysters, Turtle Soup (spiked with sherry) and Cast Iron Seared Foie Gras. You can't leave without trying the bread pudding soufflé. The bar offers a creative cocktail menu with selections like the Vieux Carre Cocktail. The white-glove service is impeccable.

THE COMPANY BURGER
4600 Freret St, New Orleans, 504-267-0320
www.thecompanyburger.com
CUISINE: Burgers/Fast Food
DRINKS: Full Bar
SERVING: Lunch, Dinner
PRICE RANGE: $$
NEIGHBORHOOD: Uptown
As the name suggests, this place specializes in burgers of the thin patty type cooked on a griddle. They are really juicy and tasty. They have a selection of great burgers served with homemade condiments.

There's also the "Curewich," nicknamed for the nearby bar **CURE**, because so many of the staff order it: it's a grilled cheese with bacon and egg. The owner's mother bakes the delicious desserts.

COMPERE LAPIN
535 Tchoupitoulas St, New Orleans, 504-599-2119
www.comperelapin.com
CUISINE: American/Caribbean
DRINKS: Full Bar
SERVING: Lunch & Dinner
PRICE RANGE: $$$
NEIGHBORHOOD: Warehouse District
Located in The Old No. 77 Hotel & Chandlery, Chef/Owner Nina Compton's menu features a combination of Caribbean, French, and Italian influences. (She's from St. Lucia and her grandmother was British.) Menu favorites include: Curried Goat and Broiled Shrimp.

THE COUNTRY CLUB
634 Louisa St, New Orleans, 504-945-0742
www.thecountryclubneworleans.com
CUISINE: American/Southern
DRINKS: Full Bar
SERVING: Lunch, Dinner
PRICE RANGE: $$
NEIGHBORHOOD: Bywater
This Country Club offers a party atmosphere with a clothing optional pool and hot tub but some people go just for the delicious food. Chef Maryjane Rosas offers a menu with a variety of treats from chicken and waffles to BBQ delicacies. Menu favorites include: Honey Lamb Roast and Seared Trout with Roasted Kohlrabi. This is also a popular Brunch destination.

COURT OF TWO SISTERS
613 Royal St, New Orleans, 504-522-7261
www.courtoftwosisters.com
CUISINE: American/Southern
DRINKS: Full Bar
SERVING: Breakfast, Lunch, Dinner
PRICE RANGE: $$$
NEIGHBORHOOD: French Quarter
This venerable establishment dates back to 1832. What you want to experience here is the courtyard with its overflowing vines of wisteria creating a luscious canopy overhead. Crawfish omelets, Cajun past and Creole jambalaya are big dishes here. Their brunch consistently wins awards. A jazz band is usually working the crowd.

DAT DOG
5030 Rue Freret St, 504-899-6883
3336 Magazine St (Uptown), 504-324-2226
601 Frenchmen St (The Marigny), 504-309-3362
www.datdognola.com
CUISINE: Fast Food
DRINKS: Full Bar
SERVING: Lunch & Dinner
PRICE RANGE: $
Famous for their gourmet hot dogs (some made with crawfish and alligator) served with whatever you want on them on sourdough rolls. Toppings include guacamole, Andouille sauce, hummus, etc. Very creative hot dog menu.

THE DELACHAISE
3442 St. Charles Ave, New Orleans, 504-895-0858
www.thedelachaise.com
CUISINE: American
DRINKS: Full Bar
SERVING: Dinner
PRICE RANGE: $$
NEIGHBORHOOD: Central City/Uptown
This is a popular watering hole for preppies and hipsters who love the impressive selection of wine and beer. The menu includes favorites like Flank Steak Bruschetta and Moules et Frites. The food is really just a step up from bar fare but it's creative and tasty.

DIMARTINO'S
700 S. Tyler, Covington, 985-276-6460
www.dimartinos.com

CUISINE: Muffulettas
DRINKS: No Booze
SERVING: Lunch & Dinner
PRICE RANGE: $$
NEIGHBORHOOD: Covington
Popular eatery with counter-serve. Menu of muffulettas, po'boys, burgers, and Italian entrees. Favorites: their signature dish - DiMartino's Famous New Orleans Muffuletta and Grilled Chicken Italian Salad. Eat in or to go.

DOMENICA
123 Baronne St, New Orleans, 504-648-6020
www.domenicarestaurant.com
CUISINE: Italian/Tapas
DRINKS: Full Bar
SERVING: Lunch, Dinner
PRICE RANGE: $$
NEIGHBORHOOD: Central Business District
Located inside the Roosevelt Hotel, this John Besh restaurant offers delicious Italian fare. Menu favorites include: Roasted Carrot pizza and Rigatoni. Save room for the Gianduja Budino, a delicious dessert. You'll also find a menu of custom-brewed beers and Italian wines.

DOMILISE'S PO'BOY & BAR
5240 Annunciation St, New Orleans, 504-899-9126
www.domilisespoboys.com
CUISINE: Barbeque/Seafood
DRINKS: Beer & Wine Only
SERVING: Lunch & Dinner; closed Sun
PRICE RANGE: $$$

NEIGHBORHOOD: West Riverside; Uptown
Local counter-serve eatery offering up giant po'boys and beers makes this one of the highlights of your visit. Don't let the fact that the place needs a paint job deter you. When you get a look at the tiny kitchen here, you'll wonder how these guys turn out the wonderful food that they do in such quantities. While you can order the usual suspects when it comes to po'boys (fried oyster, fried shrimp and roast beef), I always opt for one of their other po'boys, like the cheeseburger po'boy or the smoked hot sausage. Their condiments (hot sauces, mustards, etc.) are better than average, far better.

DONG PHUONG BAKERY & RESTAURANT
14207 Chef Menteur Hwy, New Orleans, 504-254-0214
www.dpbakeshop.com
CUISINE: Vietnamese/Chinese
DRINKS: No Booze
SERVING: Lunch, Dinner
PRICE RANGE: $
NEIGHBORHOOD: East New Orleans
There are two sides to this place, the bakery side and the restaurant side. An amazing selection of baked goods and pastries on that side, while over in the restaurant, expect a large variety of Vietnamese dishes. There's quite a large Vietnamese population in NOLA, so I've listed some of the best spots. This one is good for take-out. The bakery provides breads to many local restaurants so you know it's good.

DRAGO'S SEAFOOD RESTAURANT
2 Poydras St, New Orleans, 504-584-3911
www.dragosrestaurant.com
CUISINE: Seafood
DRINKS: Full Bar
SERVING: Lunch, Dinner
PRICE RANGE: $$
NEIGHBORHOOD: Central Business District
This is a classic New Orleans seafood eatery with an impressive menu. Menu favorites include: Lobster and Shrimp & Grits. Many favor their classic oysters, and this would be a good place to savor a Crescent City specialty, **Charbroiled Oysters**, made with garlic, herbs and butter, topped with flaky parmesan and Romano cheese. The last time I was here, I easily consumed 2 dozen of these mouthwatering delicacies. There's also a gluten-free menu.

EAT
900 Dumaine St, New Orleans, 504-522-7222
www.eatnola.com

CUISINE: Creole/Cajun/Soul Food
DRINKS: No Booze
SERVING: Lunch & Dinner, weekend Brunch; closed Mon
PRICE RANGE: $$
NEIGHBORHOOD: French Quarter
This gay-operated hipster hangout is a cut above most French Quarter spots. They have updated takes on classic New Orleans dishes like BBQ shrimp, crawfish & red beans, smoked salmon atop deviled eggs. It's all in a charming brick and pale-blue dining room.

ELIZABETH'S
601 Gallier St, New Orleans, 504-944-9272
www.elizabethsrestaurantnola.com
CUISINE: Southern
DRINKS: Full Bar
SERVING: Breakfast, Lunch & Dinner; No Dinner on Sun
PRICE RANGE: $$
NEIGHBORHOOD: Bywater
This busy spot offers down-home country classics and great po' boys. Dishes are huge. Great spot for breakfast. (Order the French toast stuffed with bananas Foster, out of this world.)

EMERIL'S DELMONICO
1300 St Charles Ave, New Orleans, 504-525-4937
www.emerilsrestaurants.com
CUISINE: Cajun/Creole
DRINKS: Full Bar
SERVING: Dinner
PRICE RANGE: $$$
NEIGHBORHOOD: Mid-City; Lower Garden District

Located on the St. Charles Avenue streetcar line, this legendary eatery offers an impressive menu of Cajun and Creole dishes. Emeril pays special attention to his flagship restaurant and the menu changes 3 or 4 times a year, keeping it fresh and alive. Menu favorites include: Moulard Duck Breast and Beef & Pork Terrine. His version of the local favorite, "Dirty Rice," includes crispy pork cheek and scallions. Save room for dessert and order the Bananas Foster for two that's prepared at your table, you won't be disappointed.

GALATOIRE'S
209 Bourbon St, New Orleans, 504-525-2021
www.galatoires.com/home
CUISINE: French
DRINKS: Full Bar
SERVING: Lunch, Dinner
PRICE RANGE: $$$
NEIGHBORHOOD: French Quarter
This French eatery specializes in old-fashioned Creole cuisine. Menu favorites include: Duck Crepes and Trout Almandine Meuniere. It's a two-level restaurant with some of the upstairs rooms overlooking Bourbon Street. This place is busy but no reservations are accepted.

GAUTREAU'S
1728 Soniat St, New Orleans, 504-899-7397
www.gautreausrestaurant.com/
CUISINE: American (New) / French
DRINKS: Full Bar
SERVING: Dinner; closed Sun
PRICE RANGE: $$$
NEIGHBORHOOD: Uptown
A little secluded eatery that offers a menu of New American-French cuisine. Favorites include: Duck confit and Halibut, pork cheek with Korean chili glaze. Try their banana split – it's a winner.

GREEN GODDESS
307 Exchange Pl, New Orleans, 504-301-3347
www.greengoddessrestaurant.com
CUISINE: American/Vegetarian
DRINKS: Full Bar

SERVING: Lunch, Dinner
PRICE RANGE: $$
NEIGHBORHOOD: French Quarter
Here you'll find traditional New Orleans fare that has been influence by a variety of cultures. Menu dishes include French, Thai, Cajun and Soul. Menu also includes vegetarian and vegan options. The bar offers a creative cocktail menu and serves quality local and regional brews. Closed Monday & Tuesday.

GW FINS
808 Bienville, New Orleans, 504-581-3467
www.GWFins.com
CUISINE: Seafood
DRINKS: Full Bar
SERVING: Dinner
PRICE RANGE: $$$
NEIGHBORHOOD: French Quarter
Here you'll find the finest quality seafood from around the world. Menu favorites include: Whole

roasted Red Snapper and Blue Nose Bass from New Zealand. Try the Lobster Dumplings served with Fennel and Tomatoes and you'll be back for more. If there's room for dessert, try the individual homemade apple pie served warm and topped with vanilla ice cream. Their wine list is very impressive with more than 100 labels, most available by the glass.

GUY'S PO-BOYS
5259 Magazine St, New Orleans, 504-891-5025
No Website
CUISINE: Sandwiches/Cajun/Creole
DRINKS: No Booze
SERVING: Lunch; closed Sun
PRICE RANGE: $
NEIGHBORHOOD: West Riverside
Great place for lunch or a quick dinner. It's best to call ahead to order. Specialty – Po-boys. There are only about 15 seats so most people take their food to go. Get the grilled shrimp po'boy.

HERBSAINT
701 St Charles Ave, New Orleans, 504-524-4114
www.herbsaint.com/
CUISINE: French
DRINKS: Full Bar
SERVING: Lunch & Dinner weekdays, Dinner Sat; closed Sun
PRICE RANGE: $$$
NEIGHBORHOOD: Warehouse District
Located in a great spot with outdoor seating, this eatery offers an upscale menu of French and American cuisine. Favorites include: Louisiana

Shrimp with Rice, artichoke and Maitake and the Muscovy Duck Leg Confit, which comes with a Dirty Rice with delicious hints of citrus "gastrique." This dish has been on the menu forever, and I always get it. Delicious desserts like their Greek Yogurt Cheesecake with roasted peaches.

HIGH HAT CAFÉ
4500 Freret St, New Orleans, 504-754-1336
www.highhatcafe.com/
CUISINE: Southern
DRINKS: Full Bar
SERVING: Lunch, Dinner
PRICE RANGE: $$

NEIGHBORHOOD: Uptown
This casual neighborhood eatery offers a menu specializing in the classic food from the Mississippi Delta. Menu favorites include: Catfish (fried, of course—I don't think they could ever cook catfish any other way) and Smoked Roasted Chicken. The bar has a nice wine list and serves local draft beers and craft cocktails.

JAMILA'S TUNISIAN CAFÉ
7808 Maple St, New Orleans, 504-866-4366
http://www.jamilascafe.com/
CUISINE: Mediterranean / Tunisian

DRINKS: Beer & Wine
SERVING: Dinner, Closed Mon
PRICE RANGE: $$$
NEIGHBORHOOD: East Carrollton
Small Mediterranean eatery with a heavy Creole flair. Husband and wife team of Jamila (she cooks) and Moncef (he brags about her) create a welcoming atmosphere. My Favorites: Lamb kabobs; the incredible Lamb Sausage; Eggplant Salad; Crawfish Bisque. The couscous here is divine. Impressive wine list. Nice desserts. Family-friendly.

JOSEPHINE ESTELLE
ACE HOTEL
600 Carondelet St, 504-930-3070
http://josephineestelle.com/
https://www.acehotel.com/neworleans/
CUISINE: Italian
DRINKS: Full Bar
SERVING: Breakfast, Lunch, & Dinner
PRICE RANGE: $$
NEIGHBORHOOD: Warehouse District
Beautiful bistro-style eatery with stately columns supporting the high ceiling, this place also has a roomy bar area where I like to enjoy the Italian specialties they serve. Favorites: Waldorf Salad (you rarely see this on a menu, and this is a good rendition); Pasta with zucchini; Gemelli (octopus bolognese); Soft Shell Crab with peaches & mushrooms; and Farmer's Breakfast. Tempting dessert menu.

THE JOINT
701 Mazant St, New Orleans, 504-949-3232
www.alwayssmokin.com
CUISINE: BBQ/Southern
DRINKS: Full Bar
SERVING: Lunch & Dinner; closed Sunday
PRICE RANGE: $$
NEIGHBORHOOD: Bywater
A menu of real Western-style BBQ keeps this place packed. Great selections of pulled pork, beef brisket and chicken and ribs. If you've never tasted peanut butter pie, then you're in for a treat. (This pie turns my stomach but those who like it *rave* about the version to be found here.)

KILLER POBOYS
Erin Rose Bar
811 Conti St, New Orleans, 504-252-6745
www.killerpoboys.com
CUISINE: Sandwiches
DRINKS: Full bar

SERVING: Lunch & Dinner; closed Tues
PRICE RANGE: $$
NEIGHBORHOOD: French Quarter
Located in the back of the Erin Rose bar, this little spot sells a variety of po'boys. Favorite: Pork belly Po'boy with lime slaw. It's a real standout.

Inside at La Petite Grocery

LA PETITE GROCERY
4238 Magazine St, New Orleans, 504-891-3377
https://www.lapetitegrocery.com/
CUISINE: French Bistro
DRINKS: Full Bar
SERVING: Lunch & Dinner, Dinner only on Mon & Tues
PRICE RANGE: $$$
NEIGHBORHOOD: East Riverside

Housed in a cottage formerly a grocery store Uptown, hence the name. Here you'll find homemade Louisiana fare with a French twist. Favorites: Turtle Bolognese; Crab Beignets; Crispy Pork Belly and Steak Tartare. New Orleans inspired desserts like the Stuffed Coconut Snoball. Reservations recommended.

LENGUA MADRE
1245 Constance St, New Orleans, 504-655-1338
lenguamadrenola.com
CUISINE: Mexican
DRINKS: Full Bar
SERVING: Dinner, Closed Mon & Tues
PRICE RANGE: $$
NEIGHBORHOOD: Lower Garden District
Unique Mexican eatery offering a 5-course tasting and a la carte menus. Though a lot of prix-fixe

restaurants have a certain "air" about them, this one doesn't. Very comfortable surroundings. I always feel like I'm visiting a friend when I come here. You will, too. From the outside, it's a little rough looking, but inside is a lot snappier. My Favorites: Shrimp Reduction Amuse; the oh-so-flavorful Gulf shrimp bouillon; and Crab meat with Avocado Tostado. Wine pairing. Impressive Mexican Spirit list.

LIUZZA'S BY THE TRACK
1518 North Lopez, New Orleans, 504-218-7888
https://liuzzasbythetrack.com/
CUISINE: Cajun/Creole
DRINKS: Full Bar
SERVING: Lunch, Dinner
PRICE RANGE: $$
NEIGHBORHOOD: Mid-City

This eatery offers a New Orleans menu of Creole and Cajun with a little Italian. Menu favorites include: Shrimp, Corn & Okra Stew and Seafood Lasagna. Their po'boys are so tasty but also too large to finish. Closed Sundays.

LUCA EATS
7329 Cohn St, New Orleans, 504-866-1166
www.lucaeats.com
CUISINE: American (Traditional)
DRINKS: No Booze
SERVING: Breakfast & Lunch
PRICE RANGE: $$
NEIGHBORHOOD: Audubon
A rundown seedy little place that's nonetheless popular because it serves good food. Menu picks: Fried bell peppers & corn grits and Oreo Beignets. Try their delicious homemade chips.

LUVI
5236 Tchoupitoulas St, New Orleans, 504-605-3340
https://www.luvirestaurant.com/
CUISINE: Asian
DRINKS: Full Bar
SERVING: Dinner, Closed Sun & Mon
PRICE RANGE: $$
NEIGHBORHOOD: West Riverside
Small Asian eatery mixing Japanese and Chinese cuisines situated in a quaint cottage Uptown offering homestyle Shanghai cuisine with a twist. Favorites: Curried Dumplings and Tuna meatballs. Menu updated regularly. Reservations recommended.

MAGASIN VIETNAMESE CAFÉ
4201 Magazine St, New Orleans, 504-896-7611
No website
CUISINE: Vietnamese
DRINKS: No Booze
SERVING: Lunch, Dinner
PRICE RANGE: $$
NEIGHBORHOOD: East Riverside
This Vietnamese eater offers a variety of Pho. Menu favorites include the Filet Mignon Pho (but I like the Oxtail Pho better) and the Avocado Spring Roll. The pig belly is braised for 40 hours until it forms a thick sauce. A bare-bones eatery offering superior food.

MAHONY'S PO'BOYS & SEAFOOD
3454 Magazine St, New Orleans, 504-899-3374
www.mahonyspoboys.com
CUISINE: Cajun/Creole
DRINKS: Full Bar
SERVING: Lunch & Dinner
PRICE RANGE: $$$
NEIGHBORHOOD: East Riverside
This counter shop offers a great menu of sandwiches and po'boys and it's hard to beat this place. Two years in a row they won the Oak Street Po'boy Festival (Po'boy Preservation Festival) with a po'boy that included fried chicken livers and Creole coleslaw. The Peacemaker po'boy has fried oysters, bacon and cheddar cheese. (Feel the heart attack coming on?) Great jambalaya also, as well as fried green tomatoes with remoulade sauce. It gets busy, so don't be surprised if there's a wait.

MANNING'S
519 Fulton St, New Orleans, 504-593-8118
www.caesars.com/harrahs-new-orleans/restaurants
CUISINE: American/Sports Bar
DRINKS: Full Bar
SERVING: Lunch, Dinner
PRICE RANGE: $$
NEIGHBORHOOD: Central Business District
Located at Harrah Casino, this Sports Bar offers a menu of American favorites with some Creole classics. This is the perfect place for sports fans with more than 30 flat screen TVs and a mega-screen TV.

MANNY RANDAZZO KING CAKES
3515 N Hullen St, Metairie, 504-456-1476
www.randazzokingcake.com/
CUISINE: Bakery
DRINKS: No Booze
SERVING: 6:30 a.m. – 5 p.m.
PRICE RANGE: $$
NEIGHBORHOOD: Metairie

Bakery specializing in king cakes in a variety of flavors. Specialty cakes baked and delivered year round.

MARJIE'S GRILL
320 S Broad Ave, New Orleans, 504-603-2234
www.marjiesgrill.com
CUISINE: Southern/Asian Fusion
DRINKS: Full bar
SERVING: Lunch & Dinner; closed Sun
PRICE RANGE: $$
NEIGHBORHOOD: Tulane / Gravier / Mid-City
Casual eatery specializing in Southern Asian cuisine mixed creatively together with Gulf ingredients. Try an order of pig knuckles—salty and crispy, covered with cane syrup. There's a BBQ pit out back where a lot of the food is coal-roasted. Shrimp are coated with cornmeal before frying. Favorites: BBQ pork shoulder and Spice-rubbed Gulf fish. Happy hour 4-6 weeknights.

MAYPOP
611 O'Keefe St, New Orleans, 504-518-6345
www.maypopnola.com
CUISINE: American (New)/Dim Sum
DRINKS: Full Bar
SERVING: Lunch, Dinner
PRICE RANGE: $$
NEIGHBORHOOD: Warehouse District
Popular eatery offers a menu of Southern-Asian fusion mixed in with Creole specialties. Favorites:

House-cured meats and Red curry octopus pasta. Menu changes regularly.

MERIL
424 Girod St, New Orleans, 504-526-3745
www.emerilsrestaurants.com/meril
CUISINE: American (New)
DRINKS: Full Bar
SERVING: Lunch, Dinner
PRICE RANGE: $$
NEIGHBORHOOD: Warehouse District
Great local eatery named after owner Emeril Lagasse's daughter Meril is unlike his other spots in the city, more modern (reclaimed wood in the interior) and adventurous and allows for numerous international influences. Favorites: Fried blue crab; Buttermilk biscuit with foie gras & blackberry jam; Spanish croquettes with ham, manchego, & piquillo pepper sauce; and Korean fried chicken. Creative desserts like Banana foster cake with ice cream or the lemon ice box pie. The cocktail menu is similarly adventurous, and ingredients are top-notch. Try the classic Hemingway daiquiri, as I did.

MIMI'S IN THE MARIGNY
2600 Chartres St, New Orleans, 504-872-9868
www.mimismarigny.com
CUISINE: Tapas
DRINKS: Full Bar
SERVING: Dinner, Late night
PRICE RANGE: $$
NEIGHBORHOOD: Marigny
This great hipster dive serves a menu of tasty tapas. Menu favorites include: Goat Cheese Croquetas and Mushroom Manchego Toast. Live music.

MINT MODERN BISTRO & BAR
5100 Freret St, New Orleans, 504-218-5534
www.mintmodernbistro.com
WEBSITE DOWN AT PRESSTIME
CUISINE: Vietnamese
DRINKS: Full Bar
SERVING: Lunch & Dinner; closed Mon
PRICE RANGE: $$
NEIGHBORHOOD: Freret

A popular modern eatery offering up a menu of Vietnamese classics and other popular Asian dishes. Menu picks include: Vietnamese pork tacos and the Kim Chi Burger.

MOTHER'S RESTAURANT
401 Poydras St, New Orleans, 504-523-9656
www.mothersrestaurant.net/
CUISINE: Cajun/Creole, American (New), Soul Food, Southern
DRINKS: Beer & Wine Only
SERVING: Breakfast, Lunch & Dinner
PRICE RANGE: $$
NEIGHBORHOOD: Central Business District
This popular red-bricked cafeteria-style eatery has been dishing out Southern fare and delicious po' boys since the late 1930s. Menu favorites include all their sandwiches and the Fried chicken. On Saturday, they serve Dirty Rice a la carte or as a side with fried chicken. (Dirty rice gets its color and texture from the hearts, gizzards and livers that are chopped or minced and then reduced in a skillet before being baked with long grain rice.)

N7
1117 Montegut St, New Orleans, No phone
www.n7nola.com
CUISINE: French; some Japanese influences
DRINKS: Full bar
SERVING: Dinner; closed Sun
PRICE RANGE: $$
NEIGHBORHOOD: St. Claude / Bywater

Casual French restaurant, with the emphasis on casual. There's an old red Citroen out front in the lush garden, just to give you a reminder that we're "going French" tonight. You go in and sit at the copper-topped bar. The antiques were collected by the owners over the years. The focus is on seafood and small plates, including "can to table" items, as they have lots of fancy tinned foods—lobster rillettes from France, calamari in spicy ragout from Portugal. You get the can, a crisp baguette, put it together with some wine and you've got a fine little meal. Favorites: Sake cured salmon and Escargot tempura. Nice wine list. Courtyard dining available.

NAPOLEON HOUSE
500 Chartres St, New Orleans, 504-524-9752
www.napoleonhouse.com
CUISINE: American/Cafe
DRINKS: Full Bar
SERVING: Lunch, Dinner

PRICE RANGE: $$
NEIGHBORHOOD: French Quarter
This French Quarter historic landmark offers a Creole-Med menu with favorites like Muffalettas and Po' Boys. Now, you can get Muffuletta in any number of places in New Orleans, but it always made sense to me to eat it in a classic building that's over 200 years old. Adds a lot of atmosphere. You know what Muffaletta is, right? (It's ham, salami, pastrami, provolone and Swiss cheeses piled high on a round chewy loaf and topped with olive salad. What makes it special is that it's heated, not served cold.) If you're a fan of gin (as I am), try the classic Pimm's Cup; it's refreshing and rarely served in other places.

NOLA PO'BOYS
908 Bourbon St, New Orleans, 504-522-2639
No website
CUISINE: Seafood/Cajun/Creole
DRINKS: No Booze
SERVING: Lunch & Dinner
PRICE RANGE: $$
NEIGHBORHOOD: French Quarter
As the name states, this place sells Po'Boys and that's it. Great varieties like Fried catfish and Shrimp. Large portions.

PALM & PINE
308 N Rampart St., 504-814-6200
https://www.palmandpinenola.com/
CUISINE: Creole / Caribbean / Latin
DRINKS: Full Bar
SERVING: Dinner; Closed Tuesdays

PRICE RANGE: $$
NEIGHBORHOOD: French Quarter
Popular eatery located in an old French Quarter townhouse. They have a "tequila cart" that I am too wise to have them bring over because I know I'd get into trouble. Serves American fare with a Latin twist from a menu that changes seasonally. Favorites: Duck with mole; Apple Chorizo Chilaquiles; Boiled Peanut Salad (don't ask); Fried Chicken Livers; Braised Duck Tamal; Goat Curry. Delicious desserts like Flan with caramelized bananas.

PARASOL'S
2533 Constance St, New Orleans, 504-354-9079
No Website
CUISINE: Cajun/Creole/American
DRINKS: Full bar
SERVING: Lunch & Dinner
PRICE RANGE: $
NEIGHBORHOOD: Irish Channel
Popular among locals but the lucky tourists find their way here for the great sandwiches. You can get a half-and-half (two different sandwiches in one). Try the shrimp and catfish or the grilled chicken with fries. Note: there's a separate entrance is you're just coming to eat.

PARKWAY BAKERY AND TAVERN
538 Hagan Ave, New Orleans, 504-482-3047
www.parkwaypoorboys.com
CUISINE: Seafood/Sandwiches
DRINKS: Full Bar
SERVING: Lunch & Dinner; closed Tues
PRICE RANGE: $$$
NEIGHBORHOOD: Bayou St. John

Popular neighborhood haunt known for its classic po'boys, and though they go back as far as 1911, they didn't start serving po'boys till 1929. Katrina put the place under 6 feet of water, but it wasn't long before they reopened and were serving their signature hot roast beef po'boys. Other super po'boys are created from alligator sausage links, BBQ beef or the hot dog po'boy. There's a surf n turf po'boy which has fried shrimp mixed with the roast beef and smothered in gravy. Sounds scary, huh? Order carefully because one sandwich is good for two. The bar attracts a lively local crowd, and it's always fun here. (And you cat eat there, thus avoiding the lines.)

PASCAL'S MANALE
1838 Napoleon Ave, New Orleans, 504-895-4877
www.pascalsmanale.com
CUISINE: Cajun/Creole
DRINKS: Full Bar
SERVING: Lunch, Dinner daily except Sunday when it's closed.
PRICE RANGE: $$$
NEIGHBORHOOD: Milan

The better oyster bars in New Orleans get their oysters from their own beds. This place is one example of that practice. This family owned eatery offers a menu of classic Cajun and Creole cuisine. Menu favorites include their Original BBQ Shrimp. Reservations recommended.

PECHE SEAFOOD GRILL
800 Magazine St, New Orleans, 504-522-1744
www.pecherestaurant.com
CUISINE: Seafood
DRINKS: Full Bar
SERVING: Lunch, Dinner
PRICE RANGE: $$$
NEIGHBORHOOD: Warehouse District
Here you'll find a menu of coastal seafood made with a modern twist to old world cooking. Many of the dishes are prepared on an open hearth over hardwood coals. Menu favorites include: Grab meat and fresh oysters. If you can tear yourself away from the lovely raw bar selections, go for the Gulf wahoo prepared 3 ways: the head that comes with salsa verde; the belly, served with a soy & chili glaze; and the collar, offered with a tart pepper jelly. I've never seen a dish like this elsewhere. The owners here wanted to veer

away from the typical fried seafood joints that proliferate in New Orleans. Maybe that's why the James Beard Foundation named it one of the Best New Restaurants in 2014.

PIECE OF MEAT
3301 Bienville St, New Orleans, 504-372-2289
https://www.pieceofmeatbutcher.com/
CUISINE: Butcher
DRINKS: Full Bar
SERVING: Lunch & Dinner, Closed Tues & Wed, Lunch only on Mon
PRICE RANGE: $$

NEIGHBORHOOD: Mid-City
Butcher shop offering a menu of sandwiches, charcuterie, and house-smoked ribs. Favorites: Turkey & Ham Sandwich and the "not turkey and the wolf bologna" sandwich. Vegetarian options. Outdoor seating, but nothing fancy.

PIZZA DELICIOUS
617 Piety St, New Orleans, 504-676-8482
www.pizzadelicious.com
CUISINE: Pizza/Italian
DRINKS: Beer & Wine Only
SERVING: Lunch & Dinner, closed Monday
PRICE RANGE: $$
NEIGHBORHOOD: Bywater
Casual counter-serve eatery serving thin-crust pizza. Small menu but usually crowded.

PYTHIAN MARKET
234 Loyola Ave, New Orleans, 504-481-9599
www.pythianmarket.com
CUISINE: Food Court
DRINKS: Full Bar
SERVING: 8 a.m. – 9 p.m.
PRICE RANGE: $$
NEIGHBORHOOD: Central Business District
In what was once the heart & soul of the African-American community, in 2018 the former Pythian "social club" was reimagined as a popular food court with eateries that emphasis local traditions. There's a pleasingly wide variety of choices, including everything from Brick-oven pizza, banh mi to Lobster Ceviche. Something for everyone.

R&O'S
216 Metairie-Hammond Hwy, Metairie, 504-831-1248
www.r-opizza.com
CUISINE: Pizza/Cajun/Creole
DRINKS: Full Bar
SERVING: Lunch daily, Dinner Wed - Sat
PRICE RANGE: $$
NEIGHBORHOOD: Metairie

A family restaurant that's usually packed and, trust me, it's because of the food, not the ambiance. Favorites include: hand tossed pizzas, Italian and seafood dishes, po'boys and their famous seafood gumbo. Still, if you only have time to visit this place once, get the roast beef po'boy. The beef is so tender. The gravy is rich and dark. The po'boy bread is toasted and the combination of these simple elements is wonderful. This place is a bit noisy and the TV is on for those wanting to watch the game.

R'EVOLUTION
777 Bienville St, New Orleans, 504-553-2277
www.revolutionnola.com/
CUISINE: Cajun/Creole
DRINKS: Full Bar
SERVING: Lunch, Dinner
PRICE RANGE: $$$$
NEIGHBORHOOD: French Quarter
This beautiful and luxurious restaurant offers an impressive menu of modern variations of Louisiana fare. The dishes showcase gulf fish, game and chops, salami, potted meats and terrines and pastas. Menu favorites include the Triptych of Quail with the birds

Southern-fried and stuffed with boudin sausage. Known for their delicious sweetbreads and one of the most extensive wine lists in town.

RALPH'S ON THE PARK
900 City Park Ave, New Orleans, 504-488-1000
www.ralphsonthepark.com/
CUISINE: Cajun/Creole
DRINKS: Full Bar
SERVING: Lunch & Dinner, Dinner only on Tues & Sat.
PRICE RANGE: $$$
NEIGHBORHOOD: City Park
Located in an old 1860's house, this upscale eatery offers a classic dining experience. Menu favorites include: fried eggs with red eye gravy, whole Gulf fish, mouthwatering items like lamb ragout with cream cheese grits or turtle soup with a liberal dash of sherry. Nice wine list. Popular Sunday brunch spot.

ROOK CAFÉ
4516 Freret St, New Orleans, 618-354-8114
http://therookcafe.com/
CUISINE: Cafe
DRINKS: No Booze
SERVING: Breakfast, Lunch & Dinner
PRICE RANGE: $
NEIGHBORHOOD: Freret

Relaxed café ideal for hanging with friends or just bring a book or your laptop. Nice selection of coffees, lattes, espressos and muffins.

SABA
5757 Magazine St, 504-324-7770
https://eatwithsaba.com/
CUISINE: Mediterranean / Middle Eastern / Israeli
DRINKS: Full Bar
SERVING: Lunch, & Dinner; Closed Mon & Tues.
PRICE RANGE: $$$
NEIGHBORHOOD: Uptown
Unpretentious but still trendy casual bistro atmosphere offering a menu of Middle Eastern fare. Small plates/family style dining. Favorites: Bulgarian Feta (with preserved leeks & coriander); Blue Crab Hummus; Squash wood-roasted; Moroccan Root Vegetables; Lamb Kebab. Popular neighborhood hangout.

Exterior at Saffron's

SAFFRON
4128 Magazine St, New Orleans, 504-323-2626
https://www.saffronnola.com/
CUISINE: Indian
DRINKS: Full Bar
SERVING: Dinner, Closed Sun & Mon
PRICE RANGE: $$$
NEIGHBORHOOD: Downtown

Upscale eatery with a flattering lighting plan that makes everybody look good offering Indian cuisine with a New Orleans flair. They mix up not only local cuisines (Creole & Cajun) but also mix up Northern and Southern Indian dishes. The results are truly something different, something you don't see anywhere else in the U.S. My Favorites: Goat Masala; a Gumbo that mixes Indian with Creole cuisine; and Bombay Shrimp (in fact, any shrimp dish you get here will be special). I always get the Paneer Pudha, which is a pancake made with lentils served with date and mint chutneys. It's bursting with flavor. You must try the Ginger Crème Brûlée. Craft cocktails.

SAINT-GERMAIN
3054 St. Claude Ave, 504-218-8729
https://saintgermainnola.com/
CUISINE: French
DRINKS: Wine
SERVING: Dinner, Lunch on Sat & Sun; Closed Wednesdays
PRICE RANGE: $$
NEIGHBORHOOD: Bywater
In a funky little cottage you'll find this Paris-style wine bar (with an excellent selection of wines by the glass) that has a separate though adjacent (reservation only) dining room. Don't let the neon sign outside that reads "Sugar Park" Pizza" fool you. House made cheese and chicken liver. Menu changes daily, but whatever they serve the night you go will be superior. (Be sure to opt in for the wine pairing deal they will offer you.) The freshly baked bread will blow you away. Reservations necessary.

SAMMY'S
3000 Elysian Fields Ave, New Orleans, 504-947-0675
www.sammysfood.com
CUISINE: Peruvian

DRINKS: No Booze
SERVING: Breakfast, Lunch & Dinner; closed Sun
PRICE RANGE: $$
NEIGHBORHOOD: St. Roch
There's usually a line at the counter. Great Po'Boys and other favorites like Seafood eggplant. They have

a great fried trout po'boy distinctive for its crispy cornmeal crust. Large portions. Poker machines.

SATSUMA CAFE
7901 Maple St, New Orleans, 504-309-5557
www.satsumacafe.com
CUISINE: Bakery/Cafe
DRINKS: No Booze
SERVING: Breakfast, Lunch
PRICE RANGE: $$
NEIGHBORHOOD: Uptown, Black Pearl
This is a bakery with a great menu of sandwiches, subs, gluten-free and vegan items. Here you'll find an interesting selection of fresh juices, like the tart and sweet Popeye juice. This is a very popular lunch spot that always crowded. Excellent coffee & cappuccino.

SEAWORTHY
ACE HOTEL
630 Carondelet St, 504-930-3071
http://www.seaworthynola.com/
https://www.acehotel.com/neworleans/
CUISINE: Seafood
DRINKS: Full Bar
SERVING: Dinner, Lunch on Sat & Sun.
PRICE RANGE: $$
NEIGHBORHOOD: Old Naples
Quaint eatery opened by the Ace Hotel in an old cottage from the 1830s. You'd never know the Ace had anything to do with this place, it's so completely different. Offering an impressive menu of locally sourced oysters and seafood. Has a great long bar where it's fun to sample some of their always-changing selection of oysters and drink some wine. I put away 3 dozen at one sitting accompanied by a very nice white burgundy. The wide-planked floor and high dark doors and wood trimming give you the feeling you're in New England or a Dublin pub, especially when it's raining outside. There are some tables out back in a kind of alleyway where you sit under towering brick walls that belong to adjacent buildings. Favorites: Grilled octopus; Swordfish with sunchokes; Anchovy Toast; Coconut & pineapple gulf fish ceviche. Wine pairings.

SHAYA
4213 Magazine St, New Orleans, 504-891-4213
www.shayarestaurant.com
CUISINE: Middle Eastern/Mediterranean

DRINKS: Full bar
SERVING: Lunch & Dinner
PRICE RANGE: $$
NEIGHBORHOOD: Touro
Casual restaurant offering a menu of modern Israeli fare. The pita bread that comes from the oven is soft as a baby's pillow and the smell fills the room with a comforting aroma. Favorites: Crispy Halloumi (Peaches, Smoked Turkish Chilies, and Pecans) and Lamb Shank. Back patio.

SOBOU
310 Chartres Street, New Orleans, 504-552-4095
www.sobounola.com
CUISINE: Cajun/Creole
DRINKS: Full Bar
SERVING: Breakfast, Lunch, Dinner
PRICE RANGE: $$

NEIGHBORHOOD: French Quarter
Sobou offers a menu of comfort food with a modern twist. Menu favorites include: Crispy Oyster Taco and Crispy Chicken on the Bone. For a treat, try the Foie Gras Float or the Cherries Jubilee & White Chocolate Bread Pudding.

ST. JAMES CHEESE CO.
5004 Prytania St, New Orleans, 504-899-4737
www.stjamescheese.com
CUISINE: Cheese Shop / Sandwiches
DRINKS: Beer & Wine Only
SERVING: Lunch & Dinner
PRICE RANGE: $$
NEIGHBORHOOD: Uptown
This tiny combination sandwich shop and market offers a great selection of cheeses. The charcuterie boards are among the best in town. The crowd is trendy and fun. In good weather, try to get a seat under the shade trees in the courtyard.

SYLVAIN
625 Chartres St, New Orleans, 504-265-8123
www.sylvainnola.com
CUISINE: American/Gastropub
DRINKS: Full Bar
SERVING: Dinner
PRICE RANGE: $$
NEIGHBORHOOD: French Quarter
This small gastropub offers an inventive menu with a strong bar serving delicious creative cocktails, like the Gunshop Fizz, made with rum and ginger beer they make here on the premises. A favorite of hipsters

and foodies (and hip younger locals, who normally don't go into the French Quarter), it's also offers a nice courtyard for dining. Chef Alex Harrell offers up menu favorites like Braised Beef Cheeks, Prochetta Po'Boys and Roasted Texas Quail as well as excellent daily specials.

TABLEAU
616 St Peter St, New Orleans, 504-934-3463
www.tableaufrenchquarter.com
CUISINE: Cajun/Creole
DRINKS: Full Bar
SERVING: Lunch, Dinner
PRICE RANGE: $$$
NEIGHBORHOOD: French Quarter
Located on Jackson Square at Le Petit Theatre, this is Dickie Brennan's newest restaurant. Chef Ben Thibodeaus offers a menu showcasing regional

ingredients and classic French Creole cuisine. Menu favorites include Fried Eggplant Batons and Filet of Beef Bearnaise. There's an open kitchen in the main dining room so the guests can see the chef at work. This is a three-story restaurant with several private dining rooms and courtyard seating. Open daily with brunch served on the weekends.

TOUPS MEATERY
845 N Carrollton Ave, New Orleans, 504-252-4999
www.toupsmeatery.com
CUISINE: Cajun/Creole
DRINKS: Full Bar
SERVING: Lunch, Dinner
PRICE RANGE: $$
NEIGHBORHOOD: Mid-City
Chef Isaac Toups offers a contemporary Cajun menu inspired by deep-rooted Louisiana family traditions. Here the food is excellent with menu favorites like: Pork Chops and Short Ribs. Dessert lovers should

save room for the Doberge cake, a multi-layered sugary confection available in several flavors.

TURKEY AND THE WOLF
739 Jackson Ave, New Orleans, 504-218-7428
www.turkeyandthewolf.com
CUISINE: Sandwiches/Desserts
DRINKS: Full bar
SERVING: Lunch & Dinner; closed Tues
PRICE RANGE: $$
NEIGHBORHOOD: Lower Garden District
Funky no-frills sandwich shop with retro tables from the 1950s, weird salt shakers, etc. Menu features an inventive list of sandwiches and cocktails. Favorites: Chicken pot pie and Lamb neck roti (with cucumber and onions). The chef here is gourmet-trained, but likes things on the casual side. Very high quality food is served here.

VERTI MARTE
1201 Royal St, New Orleans, 504-525-4767
No Website
CUISINE: Sandwiches/Salad
DRINKS: Beer & Wine
SERVING: Open 24 hours
PRICE RANGE: $
NEIGHBORHOOD: French Quarter
Market and deli known for decades for its Creole inspired sandwiches. Popular stop for those out drinking all night. Favorite: Jazz po'boy made with a heaping pile of roast turkey, ham, American and Swiss cheese, sautéed mushrooms, tomatoes, Cajun

seasoned grilled shrimp and their "special" sauce. The muffuletta here (served hot or cold) has more meat than beard, which is really good.

WAYNE JACOB'S SMOKEHOUSE
769 West 5th St, LaPlace, 985-652-9990
https://wjsmokehouse.com/
CUISINE: Smokehouse
DRINKS: Full Bar
SERVING: Lunch, Dinner, Brunch
PRICE RANGE: $$
NEIGHBORHOOD: LaPlace
A bit out of the way in LaPlace, but worth the trip. Favorites: Pork Snack Sticks; Fresh Deer Sausage; Whole Smoked Chicken; Pork Loin stuffed with andouille; Smoked Sausage Philly and Spaghetti and Meatballs. Doughnut bread pudding is a must. Popular for Brunch (menu changes weekly). The Bloody Mary here is very nice.

The line at Willie Mae's

WILLIE MAE'S SCOTCH HOUSE
2401 St Ann St, New Orleans, 504-822-9503
www.williemaesnola.com/
CUISINE: Southern, Comfort Food
DRINKS: No Booze
SERVING: Breakfast, Lunch
PRICE RANGE: $$
NEIGHBORHOOD: Mid-City, Treme
Willie Mae's is known for its delicious comfort food like their America's Best Fried Chicken. The only drawback is that it's a bit out of the way. Closed Sundays.

YE OLDE COLLEGE INN
3000 S Carrollton Ave, New Orleans, 504-866-3683
www.collegeinn1933.com
CUISINE: Southern/Creole/Cajun/American
DRINKS: Full bar
SERVING: Dinner; closed Sun & Mon
PRICE RANGE: $$
NEIGHBORHOOD: Gert Town
Casual eatery with a nice menu of Southern-Creole comfort food. Favorites Crawfish and Seafood gumbo. You must try their fried bread pudding for dessert.

Chapter 5
NIGHTLIFE

WWOZ 90.7 FM
www.wwoz.org
Tune in to this radio station when you first get to town. It plays a lot of jazz & blues, but it's completely dedicated to the local music scene. A good way to find out what's going on. This will certainly get you in the right mood to party in New Orleans.

3 KEYS
THREE KEYS
ACE HOTEL
600 Carondelet St, 504-900-1180

http://threekeysnola.com/
https://www.acehotel.com/neworleans/
NEIGHBORHOOD: Downtown
Intimate venue (maybe 50 seats) offering live music. Hosts lots of free shows. Cocktails and music.

ALTO
ACE HOTEL
600 Carondelet St, 504-900-1180
https://www.acehotel.com/neworleans/
NEIGHBORHOOD: Downtown
Rooftop garden and bar. Menu of Italian salads and small plates. Cocktails, craft beer and wine. Unbelievable views of downtown. Enjoy cocktails poolside.

BAR MARILOU
MAISON DE LA LUZ
544 Carondelet St, 504-814-7711
https://www.barmarilou.com/
NEIGHBORHOOD: Business and arts district
Delicious creative cocktails and a small menu. Be sure to explore the lobby of this gorgeously reimagined hotel property just dripping with Southern charm. You'll wish you stayed here instead of wherever it is you're staying.

BAR TONIQUE
820 N Rampart St, New Orleans, 504-324-6045
www.bartonique.com
Popular among locals and visitors, this neighborhood bar mixes up classic cocktails with fresh ingredients. Great place to stop for a cocktail before dinner.

BJ'S LOUNGE
4301 Burgundy St, New Orleans, 504-945-9256
No Website
NEIGHBORHOOD: Bywater
If you like crowded smoke filled dive bars, this is your place. It's usually packed with locals who know each other. There's live music on Monday nights featuring bands like King James and the Special Men. Free red beans & rice on Mondays. Pool tables. Cash only.

BUD RIP'S
900 Piety St, New Orleans, 504-945-5762
No Website
NEIGHBORHOOD: Bywater
This is just a classic neighborhood bar with TVs being the only frills. Some call it a dive bar, but they still show up for happy hour. There is also a pool table, dartboard and video poker. Smoking allowed.

CANDLELIGHT LOUNGE
925 North Robertson St, New Orleans, 504-957-4459
No Website
NEIGHBORHOOD: Treme
This popular Jazz & Blues Club happens to be a favorite stop for the secodline parades and the Treme Brass Band makes a stop here every Wednesday night and takes the stage. Cheap drinks and very friendly crowd. Cover on Wednesday nights.

CAROUSEL PIANO BAR & LOUNGE
Hotel Monteleone
214 Rue Royal, New Orleans, 504-523-3341
www.hotelmonteleone.com/new-orleans-dining-entertainment/carousel-bar-lounge/
NEIGHBORHOOD: French Quarter
Here you can enjoy live jazz, blues, a mint julep, and people watch without moving as it's the only revolving bar in New Orleans. Located in the **Hotel Monteleone** overlooking Royal Street. This is a long-time favorite of locals and tourists who love to sit at the 24-seat revolving carousel bar. They've expanded the place so now there's a split-level viewing area as well as street level views.

CURE
4905 Freret St, New Orleans, 504-302-2357
www.curenola.com
NEIGHBORHOOD: Freret, Uptown
This is an unpretentious (although very hip) cocktail bar located in a repurposed firehouse on a dark corner that offers a creative menu of bar snacks. Not just a place to drink, but also a place to relax and enjoy the experience. Great selection of cocktails that have been designed by serious mixologists with a strong emphasis on the house-made bitters. The cocktail menu changes 8 times a year. Bar menu features items like Steak Tartare, Jamaican meat pies, baked crabcakes and Maitake Mushrooms. This was probably New Orleans's first craft cocktail bar, but there are numerous others ones now.

D.B.A.
618 Frenchman, New Orleans, 504-942-3731
www.dbaneworleans.com
NEIGHBORHOOD: Marigny
This live music club offers a roster of local and regional acts. The bar serves beer, wine and spirits in a smoke-free environment. Cover charge.

ELYSIAN BAR
HOTEL PETER & PAUL
2317 Burgundy St, 504-356-6769
https://www.theelysianbar.com/
NEIGHBORHOOD: Faubourg Marigny District
Chic hotel bar in what was an old rectory where they put a lot of work into the décor—gingham, rattan

furniture, glittering sconces, all coming together to throw off a very 19th Century atmosphere. Has a very nice food menu, from the Grilled Okra and Crispy Eggplant to the Crispy Beef Cheeks and a Duck Egg Omelette that really hits the spot. Creative and classic cocktails. Charming atmosphere, even out in the aged-brick courtyard where you sit beneath the old stained-glass windows from the church.

FRENCH 75 BAR
813 Bienville St, New Orleans, 504-523-5433
www.arnaudsrestaurant.com/french-75
NEIGHBORHOOD: French Quarter
This is a very popular New Orleans bar but it also gets pretty smoky. The drinks are top notch and the crowd is interesting as this is a side bar to Arnaud's, one of the great dining spots of the French Quarter. Try their Herbsaint Frappe, which might be called the

mojito for New Orleans, but flavored with anise liqueur.

HI-HO LOUNGE
2239 St Claude Ave, 504-945-4446
www.hiholounge.net
NEIGHBORHOOD: St Roch
This neighborhood bar is also a live music venue that has been one of the pioneers in the underground alternative music scene. The variety of music includes indie rock, hip hop, electronic, jazz, funk and jam music. Other entertainment offered includes burlesque performances, comedy acts, and film screenings. No smoking allowed. Daily food specials offered and a guy cooks BBQ out front.

JEAN LAFITTE'S OLD ABSINTHE HOUSE
240 Bourbon St, New Orleans, 504-523-4640
www.ruebourbon.com
NEIGHBORHOOD: French Quarter
Built in 1807 as a corner grocery, this landmark saloon has become a must-see destination for locals and tourists. Unique round bar seating. Large cocktail selection. No food but they have free popcorn and an inexpensive juke box.

LATITUDE 29
BIENVILLE HOUSE
321 N Peters St, New Orleans, 504-609-3811
www.latitude29nola.com
NEIGHBORHOOD: French Quarter
A Tiki-style gastropub with a great bar menu of exotic cocktails located in the Bienville House which

dates back to the 1830s. Locals' hangout. There's a lovely courtyard with a pool. A place to get away from the noise and mayhem one usually finds in the French Quarter. Ask about the great cocktails not on the menu.

LOA
221 Camp St, New Orleans, 504-553-9550
www.ihhotel.com
Located in: International House
Popular New Orleans watering hole frequented by local artists, business owners and tourists. Located in the International House Hotel, this bar serves up a great selection of handcrafted cocktails, classics, and made to order concoctions.

Maple Leaf

MAPLE LEAF BAR
8316 Oak St, New Orleans, 504-866-9359
www.mapleleafbar.com
NEIGHBORHOOD: Uptown
This is dive live music venue is one of the longest operating music clubs in New Orleans. Live music 7 nights a week and they feature every music genre including blues, funk, R&B, rock, zydeco, jazz and jam bands with a schedule that includes local performers and touring national acts.

MARKEY'S BAR
640 Louisa St, New Orleans, 504-943-0785
www.markeysbar.com
NEIGHBORHOOD: Bywater
This friendly neighborhood bar specializes in beer on tap and good bar food. This is a local hangout for watching the game serving up about 15 beers on tap. There are 8 TVs that play a variety of sports games.

MIMI'S IN THE MARIGNY
2600 Chartres St, New Orleans, 504-872-9868
www.mimismarigny.com
NEIGHBORHOOD: Marigny
The DJ here plays a lot of old New Orleans "swamp music." There's a soul funk dance party on Saturday night.

OAK
8118 Oak St, New Orleans, 504-302-1485
www.oaknola.com
NEIGHBORHOOD: Uptown
This place offers an impressive selection of wines with nearly a hundred hand-selected bottles. The

bartenders serve some great signature cocktails. Live music consists of jazz, acoustic folk or R&B. Full menu available.

PIRATE'S ALLEY
622 Pirates Alley, New Orleans, 504-524-9332
www.piratesalleycafe.com
NEIGHBORHOOD: French Quarter
Cozy little bar that opens very early (for those that need a rum before 10 a.m.) Serving great cocktails including Absinthe, served the traditional way with the absinthe water fountain, sugar cube and slotted spoon. Cash only.

ROCK 'N' BOWL
3016 S Carrollton Ave, New Orleans, 504-861-1700
www.rocknbowl.com
CUISINE: Bowling
DRINKS: Full bar
SERVING: Lunch & Dinner; closed Sun
PRICE RANGE: $$$
NEIGHBORHOOD: Gert Town
Bowling alley, bar, and stage for live music. Great selection of music. Menu is typical bar grub.

SAINTS & SINNERS
627 Bourbon St, New Orleans, 504-528-9307
http://saintsandsinnersnola.com
NEIGHBORHOOD: French Quarter
Channing Tatum's trendy two-level lounge with an old-time bordello feel. Don't expect to see Mr. Channing, even though it's usually filled with ladies hoping he'll make an appearance. Live DJ. Nice bar grub menu featuring favorites like Alligator tacos and gumbo fries.

SNAKE AND JAKE'S CHRISTMAS CLUB LOUNGE
7612 Oak St, New Orleans, 504-861-2802
www.snakeandjakes.com
NEIGHBORHOOD: Uptown
This is a small, neighborhood bar that great for late nights. It's been voted "New Orleans Best Dive Bar" many times and has a loyal following. Music provide by the jukebox. Smoking allowed.

SPOTTED CAT MUSIC CLUB
623 Frenchman, New Orleans, 504-943-3887
www.spottedcatmusicclub.com
NEIGHBORHOOD: Marigny

This live jazz bar is a favorite among the locals. The performers often ask people onstage to dance but there's also a small dance floor.

ST. ROCH TAVERN
1200 St Roch Ave, New Orleans, 504-945-0194
No Website
NEIGHBORHOOD: St Roch
This popular dive has a welcoming neighborhood feel with cheap drinks and a tasty bar menu. On Saturday nights there's a punk rock dance party that's become legendary. It's been called the sweatiest sissy bounce party in town. Cash only.

THE SWAMP
516 Bourbon St, New Orleans, 504-231-8519
www.bourbon-swamp.com
NEIGHBORHOOD: French Quarter
Popular nightspot with a gator theme and neon lights that features a mechanical bull in the courtyard. Wrap-around balcony typical of New Orleans. Upstairs, downstairs and outdoor patio filled with a young, attractive crowd. Offers great deals like 3 for 1 beers. Try the Swamp Juice – a giant cocktail of questionable ingredients, but it packs a punch.

THREE MUSES
536 Frenchmen St, New Orleans, 504-252-4801
www.3musesnola.com/
NEIGHBORHOOD: Marigny
This relaxed nightspot offers a great mix of music and cocktails. It's a locals' hangout and is usually crowded. This is another haunt for those who like specialty cocktails, like the Spaghetti Western (bourbon, orange Campari & rosemary syrup). If you want a table, be prepared to wait. Food available. No smoking.

TWELVE MILE LIMIT
500 S Telemachus St, New Orleans, 504-488-8114
www.twelvemilelimit.com
NEIGHBORHOOD: Mid-City
What other bar offers a haircut and a cocktail for $10 (Sundays only)? This unusual nightspot offers free food on Mondays and there's a live dating show on the last Thursday of the month. This dog-friendly bar features a pool table, craft cocktails, a menu heavily tilted toward BBQ and gourmet desserts (like the excellent doberge cake). The Great Idea cocktail is a mixture of vodka, amara and ginger beer. Smoking on the patio.

VITASCOPE HALL
601 Loyola Ave, New Orleans, 504-561-1234
www.neworleans.hyatt.com/en/hotel/dining/VitascopeHall.html
NEIGHBORHOOD: French Quarter
Named after the world's first for-profit movie theater in New Orleans, this place features 42 flat screen TVs and its own iPhone and Android application to keep guests up to date. One of the best bars in New Orleans with quite an active nightlife scene. Specialty cocktails stand out here, like the Praline Sling, their version of the Sazerac, made with bourbon, pecan bitters, absinthe and caramel.

Chapter 6
WHAT TO SEE & DO

THE ALLWAYS LOUNGE & THEATRE
2240 St. Claude Ave, New Orleans, 504-321-5606
www.theallwayslounge.net
NEIGHBORHOOD: Marigny
Similar to Berlin in the 1930s, this combination lounge and theater offers a variety of theatrical

experiences including local indie, avant-garde and art. Here you'll see a variety of performers including: musicians, burlesque dancers, clowns, artists, and jacks-of-all-trades. In the rear, the 100-seat **All Ways Theatre** offers a schedule of weekend plays and other performances.

AUDUBON AQUARIUM OF THE AMERICAS
1 Canal St, New Orleans, 504-565-3033
www.auduboninstitute.org/visit/aquarium
NEIGHBORHOOD: Central Business District
ADMISSION: Modest Fee
Located on the Mississippi River adjacent to the French Quarter, the Audubon Aquarium of the Americas is a celebration of the underwater world. The colors of a Caribbean reef decorated the walk-through tunnel The venue features 10,000 animals representing 530 species like penguins, Southern sea otters, sting rays, gigantic sharks, and other fish many swimming in the 400,000 gallon Gulf of Mexico Exhibit. The Amazon exhibit, a climate-controlled greenhouse, includes macaws, piranhas, an anaconda, and freshwater stingrays. The aquarium also includes an IMAX theater.

AUDUBON PARK
6500 Magazine St, New Orleans, 504-861-2537
www.auduboninstitute.org/audubon-park
NEIGHBORHOOD: Uptown
Located approximately six miles west of the center of New Orleans, this city park was named after artist and naturalist John James Audubon. The park is bordered by the Mississippi River on one side and St. Charles

Avenue on the other. The park features a sports field and picnic facilities along the Mississippi River, a golf course, the Audubon Zoo, horseback riding, a 1.8 mile hiking, biking & jogging trail and a public swimming pool. Just about the perfect park anywhere.

BACKSTREET CULTURAL MUSEUM
1116 Henriette Delille St, 504-657-6700
www.backstreetmuseum.org
NEIGHBORHOOD: Treme
HOURS: Open daily except Sundays.
COST: Minimal fee
Small museum that features Mardi Gras costumes painstakingly sewn by hand, photos and videos. If you've never been to New Orleans during Mardi Gras, you can see what some of the more elaborate consumes look like by dropping in here. The museum also hosts public performances of music and dance.

BLAINE KERN'S MARDI GRAS WORLD
1380 Port of New Orleans Pl, New Orleans, 504-361-7821
www.mardigrasworld.com
NEIGHBORHOOD: Lower Garden District
ADMISSION: Nominal fee

If you can't visit New Orleans during Mardi Gras, then Mardi Gras World is the next best thing. You can experience "Fat Tuesday" all year long here. Tours begin every half hour, and run for about one hour. First you'll get an overall history of Mardi Gras before the guides take you through the float den, where artists work year-round to build the incredible floats and props used in the parade. This is really a behind-the-scenes look at Mardi Gras. Don't forget to take your camera as there is a lot to photograph.

BUG APPETIT
423 Canal St, New Orleans, 800-774-7394
https://audubonnatureinstitute.org/bug-appetit
NEIGHBORHOOD: Central Business District
Here's your chance to eat bugs. Insects are a great source of protein and many cultures think insects are a culinary delicacy. Here visitors can watch chefs incorporate bugs into their cooking and even sample some of the exotic creations at the Bug Appétit Buffet. See this cooking show and cultural café at the **Audubon Insectarium** where you can find fried worms in cinnamon sugar and roasted crickets on chocolate chip cookies. Try some crispy Cajun crickets. Kids love this attraction because they get to stroke the backs of beetles and cockroaches. One of the more interesting exhibits is the underground gallery where you can get a perspective of what the world looks like if you were a bug. There's also an Asian-inspired garden with thousands of butterflies.

FRENCH MARKET
1008 N Peters St, New Orleans, 504-636-6400
www.frenchmarket.org
NEIGHBORHOOD: French Quarter
The French Market is a fun outdoor shopping experience and you'll find lots of used, vintage and consignment items, handmade items, fresh produce, as well as many unusual gifts. At the Market you'll get to see live music performed outdoors, street performers and the home of the Historic Jazz Society.

FRENCH QUARTER FESTIVAL
400 N Peters St #205, New Orleans, 504-522-5730
www.fqfi.org
NEIGHBORHOOD: French Quarter
Founded in 1983, this annual music festival (DATES ARE IN APRIL) showcases some of New Orleans' best musical talent from a variety of genres including: traditional and contemporary jazz, Cajun-Zydeco, world, blues, rock, and pop. The festival also features cuisine from some of New Orleans' finest restaurants at the "World's Largest Jazz Brunch." The French Quarter Festival is the largest free music festival in the United States.

THE FRONT GALLERY
4100 St. Claude Ave, 504-301-8654
www.nolafront.org
NEIGHBORHOOD: Bywater
This artist-run collective and not-for-profit gallery offers a roster of exhibitions, lectures, screenings, performances, and additional arts programming.

Founded by artists, the front has 4 rooms that are used by the 14 members for the exhibition of their work or other invited artists. The Front promotes new and experimental work from emerging arts, both locally and internationally known.

FULTON ALLEY
600 Fulton St, New Orleans, 504-208-5593
www.fultonalley.com
NEIGHBORHOOD: Warehouse District
Upscale bowling lanes popular as much for the menu of Southern fare and cocktails. The upscale crowd reclined on tufted leather couches eating deviled eggs and pork belly sliders. Set in a beautifully redesigned bus barn and ground floor parking garage.

GAY HERITAGE TOUR
909 Bourbon St, French Quarter, New Orleans
Contact Roberts Batson @ 504-945-6789
No Website
NEIGHBORHOOD: French Quarter
ADMISSION: $20
This French Quarter walking tour – appointment only – showcases New Orleans' unique LGBT history and culture. Tour is led by Roberts Batson a celebrated historian of New Orleans' gay culture.

GOOD CHILDREN GALLERY
4037 St. Claude Ave, New Orleans, 504-975-1557
www.goodchildrengallery.com
NEIGHBORHOOD: Bywater/St Claude Arts District

This artist-run space exhibits engaging work by local, national, and international artists. The gallery is open Saturday and Sunday, 12 – 5 p.m.

HERMANN-GRIMA HOUSE MUSEUM
820 St. Louis St, New Orleans, 504-525-5661
www.hgghh.org
NEIGHBORHOOD: French Quarter
Built in 1831, the Hermann-Grima House is one of the most significant homes in New Orleans. Step back in time as you visit this handsome Federal mansion with a courtyard that is the only horse stable and functional 1830s outdoor kitchen in the French Quarter. Here you'll learn about the architecture and the Golden Age of New Orleans. This mansion has been restored to its original splendor and depicts the gracious life a prosperous Creole family of 19th

century New Orleans. The mansion is open for tours daily except for Wednesday and Sunday.

HOGS FOR THE CAUSE
www.hogsforthecause.org
NEIGHBORHOOD: City Center
This annual fundraising music and food festival raises money for pediatric brain cancer care. Every year over 80 teams compete for the title of Louisiana Pork Champion. The Friday night event has been called the "wildest outdoor cocktail party in New Orleans." Three bands play on the main stage while the teams are busy preparing their BBQ. On Saturday night guests sample the BBQ while 10 bands perform throughout the day. Check the website for dates and schedule.

JACKSON SQUARE
700 Decatur St, New Orleans, 504-658-3200
www.experienceneworleans.com/jackson-square.html
NEIGHBORHOOD: French Quarter
Located in the French Quarter, this historic park was named in honor of the Battle of New Orleans hero Andrew Jackson. This space was once going to be paved over to make way for a highway, but a huge public outcry saved it. It was once a military parade ground. The park faces the Mississippi River and is surrounded by historic buildings such as the **St. Louis Cathedral** (the oldest continuously operated cathedral in the U.S.), and the **Presbytere** and **Cabildo**, which was the center of government when New Orleans was a French colony. Local artists frequent the park to pain, draw, and display their

work. Stop by the famous **Café du Monde** for beignets with powdered sugar and café au lait. Sit under the green awning that overlooks Jackson Square. 800 Decatur St., www.cafedumonde.com

KAYAK TOURS
3494 Esplanade Ave, New Orleans, 985-778-5034
www.kayakitiyat.com
NEIGHBORHOOD: Mid-City
Take this tour led by local guides who know the area well. Tours are offered from two to four hours kayaking to various areas of the Bayou. One tour paddles the entire length of the Bayou. This is a unique way to view the community and a great opportunity for bird watching. Kayaking experience is not necessary for these tours.

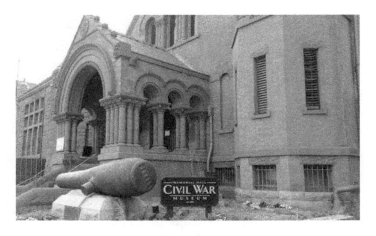

LOUISIANA'S CIVIL WAR MUSEUM
929 Camp St, New Orleans, 504-523-4522
www.confederatemuseum.com
NEIGHBORHOOD: Warehouse Arts District

ADMISSSION: Minimal fee
Formerly known as the **Confederate Museum**, this museum boasts one of the largest collections of Confederacy-related artifacts and memorabilia in the United States. Built in 1891, the cathedral-like appearance of the building contrasts to the more recent buildings in the district. On the front terrace, a large Columbiad, a Civil War-era cannon, is mounted marking the entrance of the museum. Inside the museum are Civil War uniforms worn by officers, Confederate weapons, exhibits relating to the life of Confederate soldiers, personal belongings of Confederate Generals Robert E. Lee, P.G.T. Beauregard, Braxton Bragg and Franklin Gardner, battle flags of Confederate regiments, paintings, prints, photographs and documents relating to the Civil War.

MAGAZINE STREET
www.neworleans.com/plan/streets/magazine-street/
NEIGHBORHOOD: Lower Garden District
This six-mile stretch of Garden District and Uptown thoroughfare includes a wonderful sampling of great antique shops, art galleries, craft shops and upscale boutiques. Named for a "magazine," a warehouse that was built in the late 1700s to house products waiting to be exported. The street also boasts great examples of eclectic architecture including the large columned Greek Revival houses of the mid-19th Century and colorful Victorian cottages.

MARIE LAVEAU'S HOUSE OF VOODOO
739 Bourbon St, New Orleans, 504-581-3751

www.voodooneworleans.com
NEIGHBORHOOD: French Quarter
This unique shop offers a variety of items that help aid in learning and practicing spiritual and religious ceremonies. Here you'll find tribal masks and statues, talismans, and charms. Psychic and spiritual readings available daily.

MOJO COFFEEHOUSE
1500 Magazine St, New Orleans, 504-525-2244
https://mojocoffeehouse.com/
NEIGHBORHOOD: Lower Garden District
Bohemian coffeehouse with variety of coffees and espressos, and premade snacks. This coffee is locally roasted and most people who taste it think it's the best in town. Excellent breakfast burrito. Emphasis on freshness. Lemons for the lemonade you order will be squeezed while you watch. Free Wi-Fi.

MUDLARK PUBLIC THEATER
1200 Port St, New Orleans, 504-568-2022
http://mudlark-theater.edan.io/
NEIGHBORHOOD: St. Claude
If you looking for cutting-edge theater and over the top performances, then check out the shows at this black box performance space. This theater features cutting-edge performances from some of the best and edgiest performers from all over the U.S. Also home to Big Dick's House of Big Boobs DIY strip club. Get there early to snag one of the 20 seats.

NATIONAL WORLD WAR II MUSEUM
945 Magazine St, New Orleans, 504-528-1944
www.nationalww2museum.org
NEIGHBORHOOD: Central Business District
ADMISSION: Nominal fee

This museum, formerly known as the National D-Day Museum, celebrates the American experience during World War II, particularly the Battle of Normandy. This museum has several permanent galleries and exhibitions including a Supermarine Spitfire, Messerschmitt Bf 109, Douglas SBD Dauntless dive bomber, and Douglas C-47 Skytrrain.

In the **Victory Theatre**, there's a movie the kids will enjoy (and so will you) about the war. It's narrated by Tom Hanks, and features Tobey Maguire, Brad Pitt and Kevin Bacon. During the screening, it actually snows within the theatre and the seats rattle and shake during the bombings.

The **Train Car Experience** uses a 26-seat replica of a passenger Pullman sleeping car from the 1940s. The idea is to give you a feeling for what it was like for soldiers to leave home. Big band music and film clips from the era are used to give you a unique feeling.

The museum's largest building features the newest exhibit, The **US Freedom Pavilion**: The **Boeing Center**. You should allow for approximately 3 hours for a tour of the museum.

NEW ORLEANS AIR LIFT
4557 N. Rampart St., New Orleans, No Phone
www.neworleansairlift.org
NEIGHBORHOOD: St Claude
Described as part musical playground and part music venue, this is an ongoing project to mix music with architecture. This is a landmark village of musical, playable houses with instruments embedded into the walls, ceilings and floors.

NEW ORLEANS CULINARY BIKE TOUR
634 Elysian Fields Ave, New Orleans, 504-400-5468
www.Confederacyofcruisers.com
NEIGHBORHOOD: Marigny
Bike enthusiasts enjoy this tour but it's really a great way to see New Orleans as you ride all over the city. It's an easy ride and the bikes are beach cruisers. The tour covers several neighborhoods and visit many different historic spots. Not only is this tour visual but also the tour includes a variety of tastings including snowballs, gumbo, fried oyster po' boy, pork boudin and crawfish. This tour is not for "faint stomachs" as the tour lets the riders eat New Orleans style, which means pigs and seafood. Tours are small groups. Tour price includes food and tips. Tours by reservation only.

NEW ORLEANS JAZZ & HERITAGE FESTIVAL
365 Camp St #2250, New Orleans, 504-410-4100
www.nojazzfest.com
NEIGHBORHOOD: Mid-City
One of the most anticipated events of the year, this annual celebration of New Orleans music and culture brings together every style of music associated with the city. The festival celebrates jazz, blues, R&B, gospel music, Cajun music, zydeco, Afro-Caribbean, folk music, Latin, rock, rap, country, and bluegrass. The festival also includes areas of craft booths including the Congo Square African Marketplace, Contemporary Crafts, and the Louisiana Marketplace. Another popular aspect of the festival is the parades that are held throughout the event. This festival runs for two weekends during the hours of 11 a.m. and 7 p.m. This festival is a major New Orleans tourist destination rivaled only by Mardi Gras, so expect humongous crowds.

NEW ORLEANS MOVIE TOURS
227 Bermuda St, New Orleans, 504-520-9747
www.nolamovies.com
NEIGHBORHOOD: Algiers Point
Popular tour company offering a variety of city, neighborhood, and sightseeing tours. Sitting comfortably inside a van equipped with video screens and a good speaker system, you'll visit actual locations and watch video clips from the films as you see the locations. Pretty nifty. You'll see Vivien Leigh riding the streetcar from "A Streetcar Named Desire." And see the place in Jackson Square where Kirsten Dunst bites into someone's neck in "Interview with a Vampire," among other movies.

NEW ORLEANS MUSEUM OF ART
1 Collins Diboll Cir, New Orleans, 504-658-4100
www.noma.org
HOURS: Open daily except Sunday
ADMISSION: Minimal fee
NEIGHBORHOOD: City Park
New Orleans' oldest fine arts institution, today this museum hosts an impressive permanent collection that includes nearly 40,000 objects including French and American art, photography, and glass. The sculpture garden holds over 60 sculptures set among wandering footpaths, large trees, and reflecting lagoons.

NEW ORLEANS PHARMACY MUSEUM
514 Chartres St, New Orleans, 504-565-8027
www.pharmacymuseum.org
NEIGHBORHOOD: French Quarter

ADMISSION: Very small fee; closed Sunday & Monday

An 1823 apothecary transformed into a museum with exhibits of early medicines, superstitious cures and questionable medical practices like bloodletting and leeches. Hand-blown apothecary bottles filled with drugs, medicinal herbs and potions used by Voodoo practitioners. Take the tour – it's worth it. There's a lush landscaped courtyard, an 1855 soda fountain, lots of fun here.

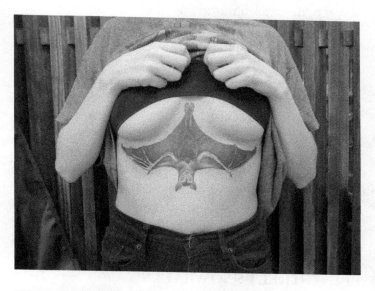

NEW ORLEANS TATTOO MUSEUM AND STUDIO
3916 St Claude Ave, New Orleans, 504-943-0409
www.nolatattoomuseum.com
NEIGHBORHOOD: Central City
ADMISSION: Donations requested

Founded to preserve and promote the history of tattooing in New Orleans. An archive of stories featuring exhibitions from well-known tattoo artists. Exhibits focus on history, technologies, traditions and influences of tattooing. The shop also specializes in custom tattoos offering the services of four award-winning artists.

OGDEN MUSEUM OF SOUTHERN ART
925 Camp St, New Orleans, LA 504-539-9650
www.ogdenmuseum.org
NEIGHBORHOOD: Central Business District
ADMISSION: Minimal fee
This museum offers collections and exhibitions that educate visitors about the visual arts and culture of the American South. The collection includes work by artists from or associated with the 15 southern states and the District of Columbia. The museum was born from the donation of more than 1,100 works from New Orleans businessman Roger H. Ogden's private collection. Now the museum holds more than 4,000 works. This collection is the largest and most comprehensive of Southern art in the world. Closed Tuesday.

PLUM STREET SNOWBALLS
1300 Burdette St, New Orleans, 504-866-7996
www.plumstreetsnoball.com/
NEIGHBORHOOD: Uptown
This colorful ice concoction is a great way to beat the heat. You might have known these as "snow cones" when you were growing up. It comes in flavors like Strawberry Shortcake, Lemonade, Bananas Foster

and even Strawberry Cheesecake. This shop, which has been here for many decades, opens seasonally in mid-March.

ROYAL STREET
NEIGHBORHOOD: French Quarter
One block off Bourbon Street, this street dates from the French Colonial era and is one of the oldest streets in New Orleans. It begins at Canal Street and runs through the French Quarter, Baubourg Marigny, Bywater and Lower 9th Ward neighborhoods to the Jackson Barracks. The section in the upper French Quarter is known for its many antique shops and art galleries. Stop in at **Goorin Brothers**, a hatmaker that's situated in an old townhouse the dates back to 1837. A section of the street between St Louis and St Ann streets is closed every afternoon to create a pedestrian mall and there you can see a variety of street performers. Royal Street is also known for its many restaurants, from the upscale **Brennan's** to the budget venues. There are also several luxury hotels on the street like the **Omni Royal Orleans** and the **Hotel Monteleone**.

SAVE OUR CEMETERIES TOURS
1539 Jackson Ave, Ste 415, New Orleans, 504-525-3377
www.saveourcemeteries.org
NEIGHBORHOOD: Treme
New Orleans' cemeteries are filled with history and legends. Take a cemetery tour and study the tombs of mayors, gamblers, jazz musicians and heroes of the War of 1812. Cemetery tours visit St. Louis Cemetery

No. 1 and Lafayette Cemetery No. 1. Each tour takes approximately 1 hour. Reservations required.

SOUTHERN FOOD & BEVERAGE MUSEUM
1504 Oretha C Haley Blvd, New Orleans, 504-569-0405
www.natfab.org
NEIGHBORHOOD: Central City
ADMISSION: Nominal fee includes admission to **The Museum of the American Cocktail**: New Orleans Collection and access to weekend programs and classes. Non-profit museum celebrates history of American Southern cuisine and cocktails. Wants to know were grits came from? Fried pickles? Boiled peanuts? Here you'll find out. Museum hosts special exhibits, demonstrations, lectures and tastings – all showcasing Southern cuisine. Attached is an authentic 1850s bar which is a fun spot to grab a bite and a cocktail.

ST. AUGUSTINE CATHOLIC CHURCH
1210 Gov. Nicholls St, New Orleans, 504-525-5934
https://staugchurch.org
NEIGHBORHOOD: Treme
Founded n 1841, this is the oldest African-American Catholic parish in the nation and was one of the first 26 sites on the states Louisiana African American Heritage Trail. This church is known for its jazz Masses and it's worth the visit just to see the choir and experience the history.

ST CHARLES AVENUE STREETCAR
www.neworleans.com/plan/transportation/streetcars/
NEIGHBORHOOD: 4 lines run throughout New Orleans
ADMISSION: Nominal fee
New Orleans is known for its streetcars, particularly the streetcar named "Desire" made famous by the Tennessee Williams play, "A Streetcar Named Desire," in which Marlon Brando so memorably screams out, "Stellaaaaa!" While the Desire line ended in the late 1940s, the streetcars still have that old world charm, with mahogany seats and shiny brass fittings as the New Orleans streetcars are one of the first passenger railroads in the US and one of the oldest operating street railways in the world. This makes a great way to enjoy the magnificent houses as you pass by under tall oak trees. Check the website for fare info and schedules.

STEAMBOAT NATCHEZ
600 Decatur St,, New Orleans, 504-569-1401

www.steamboatnatchez.com
NEIGHBORHOOD: French Quarter
ADMISSION: Price varies depending on type of cruise

Step back in time and enjoy the romance of old New Orleans aboard this authentic stern wheeler. A two-hour daytime cruise with riverfront narration offers an enjoyable journey that includes the Port and skyline of New Orleans. Onboard guests can visit the museum quality engine room and enjoy a live jazz band (seasonal). There's an evening Dinner Jazz Cruise available for a truly romantic experience. Reservations necessary.

ST. LOUIS CEMETERY NO. 1
425 Basin St, New Orleans, 504-596-3050
www.frenchquarter.com/st-louis-cemetery-no-1/

NEIGHBORHOOD: Treme
New Orleans is known for its cemeteries and this is the oldest existing cemetery in the city. You can explore the cemetery on your own or take a tour. Established in the late 1700s, this cemetery is the final resting site of many of New Orleans families.

TABASCO FACTORY
32 Wisteria Rd, Avery Island, 337-373-6129
www.tabasco.com
ADMISSION: Nominal fee
The Tabasco Factory offers a unique touring experience with a feel of the South Louisiana marshes and bayous with a natural preserve on 2,200-acre Avery Island. (You will smell the pungent aroma long before you get to the factory.) You can tour the pepper sauce factory to see how Tabasco Sauce is aged in white oak barrels. In addition to the factory, visitors can also visit the company-owned 170-acre botanical garden, **Jungle Gardens,** with its beautiful display of azaleas, camellias and bamboo. There's also **Bird City**, a huge sanctuary. Besides the beautiful flowers, you'll sometimes spot alligators, deer and raccoons that live in the hills and marshes around the gardens. There's also a Tabasco Country Store for guests to visit after the tour.

WHITNEY PLANTATION
5099 Louisiana Highway 18, Edgard, 225-265-3300
www.whitneyplantation.org/
NEIGHBORHOOD: Whitney Plantation Historic District
HOURS: Open daily except Tuesdays.

COST: Minimum fee for hour and half tour/Advance tickets recommended

Plantation is a museum of slavery located on the grounds of a plantation where sugar, rice and indigo were raised. In an interesting twist, and a nod to the times (that means "identity politics"), the tour emphasizes not lives of the folks who lived in the big white mansion, but the slaves who worked the fields. I wish they'd do this more in places like Newport, where you'd see what it was like to be a servant working for the Vanderbilts. Located an hour's drive from New Orleans – there is no public transportation to the museum. However, several tour companies offer transit services daily.

Memorial to slaves killed in an uprising.

Chapter 7
SHOPPING & SERVICES

BACCHANAL WINE
600 Poland Ave, New Orleans, 504-948-9111
www.bacchanalwine.com
NEIGHBORHOOD: Bywater
This eclectic little wine shop, with a big backyard and a treehouse, is also a wine bar, a live music venue, New York style deli, and an international deli. Check out the delicious eats from Chef Joaquin Rodas. Open from 11 a.m. to midnight, seven days a week. Live music in the courtyard seven nights a week, weather permitting.

CENTRAL GROCERY
923 Decatur St, New Orleans, 504-523-1620
http://centralgrocery.com/
NEIGHBORHOOD: French Quarter
Small Italian hole-in-the-wall market selling specialty foods and sandwiches since 1919. (They serve between 300 to 500 sandwiches a day, all cold.) You'll see an assembly line layout where staff put together sandwiches in layers: Genoa salami, Holland ham, mortadella, their own olive salad, Swiss cheese and provolone all piled onto an 8-inch round of bread. Some even say the Muffuletta was invented here. (They do not discourage this rumor.) Large variety of condiments – like Wiggle's pickles. If you can get one of the 40 stools, you can eat here. Otherwise, go across to the Woldenberg Park overlooking the Mississippi.

DOMINO SOUND RECORD SHACK
2557 Bayou Rd, New Orleans, 504-309-0871

www.dominosoundrecords.com
NEIGHBORHOOD: Seventh Ward
If vinyl is your thing then this is your place. This shop offers an impressive selection of vintage world, blues, gospel, punk, avant classical, zydeco, R&B and local records. Here you'll also find cassettes, dominoes, and some stereo equipment. Cash only.

KEIFE & CO.
801 Howard Ave, New Orleans, 504-523-7272
www.keifeandco.com
NEIGHBORHOOD: Warehouse District
This is a lot more than a truly wonderful store in a building with floor-to-ceiling wooden shelves groaning with bottles of wine from hundreds of vineyards around the world. They also have imported

French mustards, Parisian caramels and artisanal olive oils and vinegars. It feels like a cross between a really neat store, a wine bar and a library, believe it or not. But since it is in the artsy Warehouse District, it all makes sense. Great place to stop in to get a gift.

MAGAZINE ST. BARBER SHOP
4224 Magazine St, New Orleans, 504-267-7823
www.magazinestbarbershop.com
NEIGHBORHOOD: East Riverside
This is an old school barbershop where you can get "the best shave across the planet." There are only three chairs but it's worth the wait. This barbershop has been around for decades. It's probably the best shave in the Crescent City. I stop in here after a long night out and the minute they drop that hot steamed towel over my face, I feel better. After the shave, I feel like I can do all the things I shouldn't have done last night again tonight.

MAURICE FRENCH PASTRIES
3501 Hessner Ave, Metairie, 504-885-1526
www.mauricefrenchpastries.com
NEIGHBORHOOD: French Quarter
This pastry shop boasts two locations, both in Metairie. Owned by Jean-Luc Albin, this shop offers a great selection of pastries, pies, and cakes. You'll find delicious items like chocolate and lemon doeberge, special occasion cakes, and party treats including sugar-free breads and cakes. They also make delectable *galette des roi*, or King Cake, with an almond-flavored filling.

INDEX

:

: Bakery, 75

1

1000 FIGS, 33

3

3 KEYS, 105

A

ACE HOTEL, 13, 67, 96, 105, 106
ACME OYSTER HOUSE, 34
ADDIS NOLA, 35
All Ways Theatre, 122
ALLWAYS LOUNGE & THEATRE, 121
ALTO, 106
American, 53, 82, 103
American (New, 62, 79
ANCORA PIZZERIA, 36
ARNAUD'S, 36
Asian Fusion, 76
ATCHAFALAYA, 37
AUDUBON AQUARIUM, 122
AUDUBON COTTAGES, 13
Audubon Insectarium, 125
AUDUBON PARK, 122
AUGUST, 37

B

BACCHANAL WINE, 146
BACKSTREET CULTURAL MUSEUM, 123
BAKERY BAR, 38
BAR MARILOU, 106
BAR TONIQUE, 106
Barbeque/, 56
BARROW'S CATFISH, 39
BBQ, 68
BEVI SEAFOOD CO, 40
BIENVILLE HOUSE, 111
Bird City, 143
BJ'S LOUNGE, 107
BLAINE KERN'S MARDI GRAS WORLD, 124
Boeing Center, 134
BON TON CAFÉ, 40
BORGNE, 42
BOUCHERIE, 43
BOULIGNY TAVERN, 43
BOURBON HOUSE, 44
Bowling, 114
Brennan's, 139
BRENNAN'S, 45
BRIGTSEN'S, 41
BROUSSARD'S, 46
BUD RIP'S, 107
Burgundy Bar, 25
BYWATER AMERICAN BISTRO, 46

C

Cabildo, 129

Cafe, 91
Café du Monde, 130
CAFÉ SBISA, 47
Cajun, 37, 40, 59, 74
Cajun/Creole, 64, 79, 81, 82, 88, 90
CANDLELIGHT LOUNGE, 107
CANE & TABLE, 48
Caribbean, 48, 53
Carousel Bar, 19
CAROUSEL PIANO BAR & LOUNGE, 108
CASAMENTO'S, 48
CENTRAL GROCERY, 147
Charbroiled Oysters, 58
CHARLIE'S STEAK HOUSE, 49
Cheese Shop, 98
Chinese, 73
COCHON BUTCHER, 50
Cocktail Bar at the Windsor Court, 30
COLUMNS, 14
COMMANDER'S PALACE, 51
COMPANY BURGER, 52
COMPERE LAPIN, 53
Confederate Museum, 131
COUNTRY CLUB, 54
COURT OF TWO SISTERS, 54
Creole, 37, 40, 59, 74
Creole/Cajun, 103
CURE, 109

D

D.B.A., 109
DAT DOG, 55
DELACHAISE, 55
DELMONICO, 60

Desserts, 101
DIMARTINO'S, 55
DOMENICA, 56
DOMILISE'S PO-BOY & BAR, 56
DOMINO SOUND RECORD SHACK, 147
DONG PHUONG, 57
DRAGO'S SEAFOOD, 58

E

EAT, 58
ELIZABETH'S, 59
ELYSIAN BAR, 109
EMERIL'S DELMONICO, 60
Erin Rose Bar, 68
Ethiopian, 35

F

French, 38, 64, 79
FRENCH 75 BAR, 110
French Bistro, 69
FRENCH MARKET, 126
FRENCH QUARTER FESTIVAL, 126
FRONT GALLERY, 126
FULTON ALLEY, 127

G

GALATOIRE'S, 61
GAUTREAU'S, 62
GAY HERITAGE TOUR, 127
GOOD CHILDREN GALLERY, 127
Goorin Brothers, 139

GREEN GODDESS, 62
GREEN HOUSE INN, 15
Grill Room, 30
GUY'S PO-BOYS, 64
GW FINS, 63

H

HARRAH'S NEW ORLEANS, 15
HENRY HOWARD HOTEL, 16
HERBSAINT, 64
HERMANN-GRIMA HOUSE MUSEUM, 128
HIGH HAT CAFÉ, 65
HI-HO LOUNGE, 111
HOGS FOR THE CAUSE, 129
HOTEL JUNG, 16
Hotel Monteleone, 108, 139
HOTEL PETER & PAUL, 19
HOTEL PETER AND PAUL, 109
HOUMAS HOUSE, 20

I

Indian, 93
INTERNATIONAL HOUSE, 20
Italian, 87

J

JACKSON SQUARE, 129
JAMILA'S CAFÉ, 66
Japanese, 73
Jazz Bistro, 37

JEAN LAFITTE'S OLD ABSINTHE HOUSE, 111
JOINT, 68
JOSEPHINE ESTELLE, 67
Jungle Gardens, 143

K

KAYAK TOURS, 130
KEIFE & CO., 148
KILLER POBOYS, 68

L

LA PETITE GROCERY, 69
LATITUDE 29, 111
LE MARAIS, 17
Le Salon, 30
LENGUA MADRE, 70
LIUZZA'S BY THE TRACK, 71
LOA, 20, 112
LOUISIANA'S CIVIL WAR MUSEUM, 130
LUCA EATS, 72
LUVI, 73

M

MAGASIN VIETNAMESE CAFÉ, 74
MAGAZINE ST. BARBER SHOP, 149
MAGAZINE STREET, 131
MAHONY'S PO-BOY SHOP, 74
MAISON DE LA LUZ, 21, 106
MANNING'S, 75

MANNY RANDAZZO KING CAKES, 75
MAPLE LEAF BAR, 113
MARIE LAVEAU'S HOUSE OF VOODOO, 131
MARJIE'S GRILL, 76
MARKEY'S BAR, 113
MAURICE FRENCH PASTRIES, 149
MAYPOP, 76
MAZARIN, 18
Mediterranean, 96
MERIL, 77
Mexican, 70
Middle Eastern, 96
MIMI'S IN THE MARIGNY, 78, 113
MINT MODERN BISTRO & BAR, 78
MOJO COFFEEHOUSE, 132
MONTELEONE, 18
MOTHER'S RESTAURANT, 79
MUDLARK PUBLIC THEATER, 132
Muffulettas, 56
Museum of the American Cocktail, 140

N

N7, 79
NAPOLEON HOUSE, 80
NATIONAL WORLD WAR II MUSEUM, 133
NEW ORLEANS CULINARY BIKE TOUR, 134
NEW ORLEANS JAZZ & HERITAGE FESTIVAL, 135
NEW ORLEANS MOVIE TOURS, 136
NEW ORLEANS MUSEUM OF ART, 136
NOLA PO'BOYS, 81

O

OAK, 113
OGDEN MUSEUM OF SOUTHERN ART, 138
OLD NO. 77, 22
Omni Royal Orleans, 139

P

PALM & PINE, 81
PARASOL'S, 82
PARKWAY BAKERY AND TAVERN, 83
PASCAL'S MANALE, 84
PECHE SEAFOOD GRILL, 85
Peruvian, 94
PHARMACY MUSEUM, 136
PIECE OF MEAT, 86
PIRATE'S ALLEY, 114
Pizza, 87, 88
PIZZA DELICIOUS, 87
PLUM STREET SNOWBALLS, 138
Polo Club Lounge, 30
Presbytere, 129
PYTHIAN MARKET, 87

R

R Bar, 25
R'EVOLUTION, 89
R&O'S, 88
RALPH'S ON THE PARK, 90
ROCK 'N' BOWL, 114
ROOK CAFÉ, 91
ROOSEVELT, 23
ROYAL SONESTA, 24
ROYAL STREET, 139
ROYAL STREET INN, 25

S

SABA, 92
SAFFRON, 93
SAINT, 25
SAINT-GERMAIN, 94
SAINTS & SINNERS, 115
Salad, 101
SAMMY'S, 94
Sandwiches, 40, 64, 68, 83, 98, 101
SATSUMA CAFE, 95
SAVE OUR CEMETERIES TOURS, 139
Sazerac Bar, 24
Seafood, 40, 48, 56, 81, 83
SEAWORTHY, 96
SHAYA, 96
SHERATON NEW ORLEANS, 27
SNAKE AND JAKE'S CHRISTMAS CLUB LOUNGE, 116
SOBOU, 97
SONIET HOUSE, 27
Soul Food, 59, 79
Southern, 59, 68, 76, 79, 103
SOUTHERN FOOD & BEVERAGE MUSEUM, 140
SPOTTED CAT MUSIC CLUB, 116
ST CHARLES AVENUE STREETCAR, 141
ST. AUGUSTINE CATHOLIC CHURCH, 141
ST. JAMES CHEESE CO, 98
St. Louis Cathedral, 129
ST. LOUIS CEMETERY NO. 1, 142
ST. PHILIP RESIDENCE, 26
ST. ROCH TAVERN, 117
Steakhouse, 49
STEAMBOAT NATCHEZ, 141
SWAMP, 117
SYLVAIN, 98

T

TABASCO FACTORY, 143
TABLEAU, 99
TATTOO MUSEUM AND STUDIO, 137
Tempt, 25
TERRELL HOUSE, 28
THREE KEYS, 105
THREE MUSES, 118
TOUPS MEATERY, 100
Train Car Experience, 133
Tunisian, 66
TURKEY AND THE WOLF, 101
TWELVE MILE LIMIT, 119

U

US Freedom Pavilion, 134

V

VERTI MARTE, 101
Victorian Lounge, 14
Victory Theatre, 133
Vietnamese, 78
VITASCOPE HALL, 120

W

W NEW ORLEANS, 29

WAYNE JACOB'S SMOKEHOUSE, 102
WHITNEY PLANTATION, 143
WILLIE MAE'S SCOTCH HOUSE, 103
WINDSOR COURT, 30
WWOZ 90.7 FM, 105
WYNDHAM LA BELLE MAISON, 31

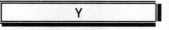

Y

YE OLDE COLLEGE INN, 103

CPSIA information can be obtained
at www.ICGtesting.com
Printed in the USA
BVHW051037060123
655734BV00013B/94